The

Hai

Wha

who

L

Carers Handbook Series

The Carer's Handbook:
What to do and who to turn to

Marina Lewycka

BOOKS

To my mother Halyna Lewycka,
and all those who cared for her

© 2004 Age Concern England
Published by Age Concern England
1268 London Road
London SW16 4ER

First published 1993 in Age Concern Books' *Caring in a Crisis* series
Second edition 1998
Reprinted 2001
Re-issued 2004

Editor Ro Lyon
Production Vinnette Marshall
Designed and typeset by GreenGate Publishing Services, Tonbridge, Kent
Printed in Great Britain by Bell & Bain Ltd, Glasgow

A catalogue record for this book is available from the British Library.

ISBN 0-86242-366-X

Contents

About the author

Marina Lewycka is a lecturer and freelance writer. She contributed to the BBC handbook *Who Cares Now?* and her training resource pack *Survival Skills for Carers* is published by the National Extension College with support from the Department of Health. She has been involved in the organisation of weekend courses for carers. She has written about care for people with learning disability and autism. She is also the author of five other books in this Carers Handbook Series.

Introduction

Most of us have to look after an older relative at some time in our lives. It often happens when we are least prepared. We may be so busy with our own jobs and families that it's easy to forget that our parents are getting older. Besides, they always seem to cope so well. Then suddenly something happens – an accident or an illness – and their world and ours is turned upside down.

If the person who needs care lives many miles away, it can be difficult to know who to contact and where to get help. Families often live far apart, and making arrangements at a distance can be an extra problem.

This book aims to help you through those first hours and days. It explains the roles of the professional workers who will look after your relative, and looks at the decisions you may have to make. It also looks at some longer-term options for the care of your relative, and the services which may be available.

The book is for anyone who suddenly finds themselves having to look after another person. That other person is perhaps most likely to be one of our parents, or a partner. But many people also find themselves looking after grandparents, an uncle or aunt, a brother or sister, or a close friend who suddenly becomes ill or has an accident. Although, for simplicity, this book talks about caring for 'your relative', you do not of course have to be related to someone to care for them.

1 Dealing with a crisis

In the past it was usually a telegram that brought bad news. Today it is more likely to be a telephone call that alerts you to a crisis. It might be a call from a relative or a neighbour, or from the hospital where your relative has been admitted.

Your relative may have fallen ill, or had an accident. Or a long-standing condition such as cancer or Alzheimer's disease may have become suddenly worse. Or the person who usually looks after your relative may have fallen ill or had an accident, leaving your relative on their own. What should you do?

Your first reaction may well be one of panic, especially if the call is unexpected or comes late at night. However upset you feel, try to keep calm. It will help you think more clearly. This chapter discusses how you can decide what needs to be done immediately and how to arrange care in an emergency.

Julie

'It was six o'clock one evening when I heard about my mother's accident. I was just getting the tea on the table. Peter had got back late and tired from work. The twins were demanding attention. It was one of those days. Then there was this phone call from the hospital in Cleveland, saying my mother had had a bad fall, and had broken her leg.

1

'I just panicked. "Right," I said, "I'm off! I've got to get up there. I'm bringing her back with me. She can't go on living alone."

'Peter calmed me down. "Sit down," he said, "and finish your tea. Let's talk this through. I've got nothing against your mother living with us, if it's the best thing for everybody. But we can't just rush into a big decision like this."

'Over tea, we talked through the possibilities. Peter said, "Why don't you phone your brother in Newcastle. It's much nearer for him. He could go up tonight, and you can go up tomorrow."

'I phoned my brother. He'd also heard from the hospital, and was just about to set off. "I'll be there in half an hour," he said, "but I can't stay next day, because of work." I said I would go up next day, and we agreed that we'd get together later on and have a talk. I arranged for a neighbour to pick the twins up from school next day, and I went up on the train.

'I was glad I phoned my brother. I'd never been very close to him, and somehow I didn't think he'd be much help. In fact, looking after mother has brought us closer together, and now we share caring for her.'

Assessing the immediate situation

If your relative, or the person who looks after them, is injured or seriously ill, there are certain decisions you will need to make immediately. Will your relative be alright on their own until you arrive or do you need to arrange for someone to sit with them until you get there? Is the situation so serious that an ambulance needs to be called? If your relative (or their carer) has had a fall or been taken suddenly ill, you will in any case want to be sure that the GP has been contacted.

Before you can make any decision, you will need to find out as much as possible about your relative's condition. When you got the initial phone call alerting you to the crisis, whether from your relative themselves or from a neighbour or even from their GP, you may well have been too shocked to ask all the questions you wanted to ask. In this case it is vital to ring back and find out more. The following are some of the things you might want to know:

- Has the doctor been called?
- If the doctor has not been called, can your relative make the call themselves or should you do it? Doctor's phone number?
- Can your relative get up from their chair or their bed – to go to the toilet; make themselves a hot drink; and to answer the door when the doctor comes?
- Is there a neighbour who could be asked to come round? Has the neighbour got a key?
- Are they feeling dizzy, breathless, drowsy or in pain?
- Are they cold? Can they, or someone else, reach enough blankets to keep them warm, or, again, can they make themselves a hot drink?
- If your relative has had a fall, are they bleeding anywhere? Do they think they have broken a bone? Can they move the affected part of their body?
- Do they feel worried about being on their own until you arrive?

If your relative cannot answer the door themselves and there isn't anyone else who has a key and can come round, the doctor will contact the police and they will break in to your relative's home. If it is a neighbour or the GP you speak to rather than your relative, then they will probably be able to reassure you on some of the points above.

If you decide you do have to arrange emergency care for your relative, see pages 4–6 for suggestions about who to contact.

Deciding what can wait

There may be major decisions to be made about where they will live and how they will be cared for. But you do not have to make all these decisions immediately. In fact, it is better to leave the big decisions until their condition has stabilised, and you have a clearer picture of how much care they will need.

Waiting a bit also gives you time to adjust to the situation. When you first see your relative, especially if they are in hospital, you may feel quite shocked and upset. It is best to try not to let this show, and remind yourself that this is a crisis, and that things can change very quickly. They may begin to look much better after they have rested for a day or two in hospital.

The long-term decisions are looked at in Chapter 5. With luck, you will have more time to make these long-term decisions, including the time to talk to everyone who could be affected. Sometimes you may feel that, under pressure, you made the wrong decision and then regret it. After an emergency, you may have to accept that the decision you made was the best you could do at the time and in the circumstances.

Arranging care in an emergency

When you hear of your relative's crisis, you may be able to just drop everything and go to them. But for some people, this is just not possible. Or you may have other commitments, which mean that you cannot stay for very long. In either case, you will need to arrange short-term emergency care, until more permanent arrangements can be made.

Listed below are some suggestions about contacts if you need to arrange care for your relative at very short notice. (Chapter 3 looks in more detail at who's who in social services and the health service.) If you live some distance away, or do not know the relevant phone numbers, you may need to go through directory enquiries to contact them.

Contacts

Other members of your family who live near your relative.

A friend or neighbour of your relative who lives close by.

Your relative's GP.

4

The community nurse (called the district nurse in some areas) – this may be difficult if it is a weekend.

The social services department in your relative's area. It may be able to do an emergency assessment (see pages 9–14) or arrange temporary care at short notice. Ask for the duty officer and explain the situation, saying that your relative needs immediate care. There should be a 24-hour emergency number.

The hospital social worker (if your relative is in hospital, but may be discharged shortly). Explain that there may be no one to look after your relative when they return home.

The Crossroads – Caring for Carers scheme in your relative's area. This is a national charity (address on page 108) which provides respite care in people's homes, and may also provide emergency care. There are charges for all services, although in some circumstances the local authority may pay some or all of the charges. Sometimes Crossroads can be contracted by the local social services department to provide emergency care.

A private agency which provides care for elderly people in their own homes and may be able to arrange for someone to sit with your relative until you arrive. You might expect to pay possibly a minimum of £10 an hour in London, for example; but fees will vary according to the services provided. The United Kingdom Home Care Association (address on page 114) should be able to tell you about agencies in your relative's area.

The local Age Concern organisation in your relative's area. It will know about any other voluntary, private or council-run care services in the area. It may also have a network of volunteer visitors who will drop in.

A nursing agency (look in the *Yellow Pages*). They can provide a trained nurse to go into your relative's home. Fees can vary widely, depending where you live.

An agency already known to your relative, for example a church or voluntary group, from which they may already be receiving support.

The ambulance service, if you think your relative may need hospital care.

The police If you cannot contact anyone else, ring the police in your relative's area, and explain the situation to them. They will know the local social services emergency procedure, and they will arrange an ambulance if necessary.

Finding out more about your relative's illness or disability

There will almost certainly be a voluntary group or charity which offers advice and information about your relative's illness or disability (see the list of useful organisations at the back of the book).

Most of these charities or voluntary organisations are national – that is, they cover the whole country – but sometimes there are also local branches. These will be listed in your telephone directory, or the national office will be able to put you in touch with local contacts.

Other people who can help

It is all too easy to feel that everything is up to you, and that you have to solve all the problems single-handed. In fact, of course, you are not on your own. Apart from other members of the family and friends, there are other people whose job it is to help, and to whom you can turn for advice and support.

Health care staff
Your relative's GP
Your own GP (if you are feeling very stressed)
Community nurse (district nurse)
Community mental health nurse
Hospital nursing staff

Social services
Social worker

Voluntary organisations
Age Concern
Local church
Local community group
Local good neighbour or befriending scheme
Carers UK
Club or society to which your relative belongs or belonged
Welfare association or trade union connected with your relative's former employment

Other people you know

_____

_____

_____

_____

You could ask the local Council for Voluntary Service or library if they know about other voluntary or self-help groups in the area.

Don't be afraid or embarrassed to ask for help. People who support carers know what a difficult and sometimes lonely task you face, and they will be only too pleased to help.

2 Arranging care for your relative

This chapter looks at how to make arrangements for your relative's care once you have made sure that they are safe, and the most immediate crisis is past. If you have not already contacted the local social services department, it may be a good idea to involve them now, to help you make whatever arrangements are necessary.

Some people are reluctant to contact social services. They think social workers are for other people, so-called 'problem families', or people with serious disabilities. They think that families should 'look after their own'. While pride and independence are very valuable qualities – a source of strength which helps many older people to keep going – they can sometimes make things unnecessarily difficult. Other older people may feel that they have contributed to society by paying tax for decades, and that they have the right in any case to be looked after in their time of need.

Ken

Ken's father went to live with Ken and Ella and their two sons when his wife died. He had had a stroke, and could only get about with difficulty. He needed a lot of looking after, including help with washing and dressing. 'Well, we didn't mind that. The problem was, Dad wouldn't let anyone apart from me and Ella do anything for him. But we were both working, and we found we just weren't giving enough time to the kids – or to each other. The social worker said we should get somebody in to help. She said they had people who would come to the house and help him with personal care. But he said, "I don't want any strangers looking after me."

'We struggled on for a bit longer, and then Ella said she just couldn't cope anymore. She said either he has someone come here to look after him, or he goes into a home. So Dad agreed, and social services sent somebody round. We thought she was really nice, but after the first time she came round Dad said she'd stolen some money, and he wouldn't have her in the house. We had a big row.

'The social worker suggested that Dad could go into a home just for a couple of weeks, to give me and Ella a break. But Dad refused to go. He said we were abandoning him. I couldn't really argue with him. He just made me feel so guilty. Then the social worker tried to talk to him, but he wouldn't listen to her either. He said she was interfering.

'In the end it was the GP who persuaded Dad to go into respite care. He explained that looking after him was a full-time job for us, and we needed a holiday. I don't know why, but Dad accepted that – maybe because the GP was a man, or maybe because he was nearer Dad's age. I think the GP pointed out that if we couldn't cope, then he might have to go into a home permanently.

'In fact he really enjoyed his two weeks away, and he talks about it all the time. You can't imagine what a difference it made to us, that two weeks' holiday.'

Now the GP has also persuaded Ken's father to let someone get him up and dress him a couple of mornings a week, and put him to bed in the evening.

Assessing your relative's needs

If your relative wants to stay at home but needs help in order to manage (or if they need to go into a care home and need help with the cost), the local social services department (called the social work department in Scotland) should carry out an **assessment**. Under the _NHS and Community Care Act 1990_, or, if your relative is disabled, under the _Disabled Persons (Services, Consultation and Representation) Act 1986_, councils have a duty to assess the needs of people who appear to need community care services.

The aim of the assessment is to identify your relative's needs and then to make a decision about what, if anything, the social services department is obliged to provide to meet your relative's assessed needs. If it is decided that the social services department will provide or arrange services, your relative will have a financial assessment to see how much they should pay towards the cost of care. The social services department is responsible for co-ordinating the assessment, but other authorities or organisations may also take part. The Government is introducing a Single Assessment Process for Older People (SAP) which will be able to combine assessment for social care needs with assessment of health care needs.

Under the _Carers (Recognition and Services) Act 1995_, if you are providing a substantial amount of care to your relative on a regular basis, you also have the right to ask the council to consider your needs when they are assessing the needs of your relative. The _Carers and Disabled Children Act 2000_ extends this right, giving you the right to have your needs assessed even if your relative does not want to be assessed. Carers UK (see address on page 107) has more information about assessment for carers and other sources of support available through carers' groups and carers' centres.

You can ask the local social services department to carry out an assessment for your relative. If your relative has given their permission, just ring up and ask for the duty officer, or for the section which deals with elderly people or their carers in your area, and explain your concerns.

The Government has given some guidance to local authorities (councils) on how to carry out assessments, but the assessment procedure will vary from area to area. More than one person could be involved in carrying out an assessment, including a social worker, a physiotherapist and an occupational therapist.

If your relative is in hospital and hasn't received a copy of the hospital discharge procedure, you should check that the hospital social services have been informed that your relative is likely to require community care support on discharge. Ask for the title, and preferably the name, of the person on your relative's ward who will be responsible for ensuring that the procedure progresses appropriately.

If you are able to organise help at home for your relative yourself, and you and/or your relative are satisfied that you able to pay for it, there is no need to involve the social services department. But it may still be worth doing, because you may find out about other services for your relative which you had not thought of. Even if you or your relative can pay for their care needs to be met, you still have the right to a free assessment.

What questions will be asked?

The assessment should look both at your relative's overall needs and at the particular problems which have led to your request for an assessment. There will usually be an initial screening (in person, or perhaps by phone) to see if your relative does need a formal assessment or to see if their needs are urgent.

If your relative has an assessment, it will be useful to have the following information to hand for the assessor, and perhaps for you and your relative to have talked through some of the issues which may arise:

Biographical details Age, family circumstances, ethnic origin, religion, etc.

What help your relative thinks they need.

How well they can manage Can they look after themselves, and cope with everyday tasks such as getting washed and dressed, eating, walking around, going up and down stairs?

Their health, both physical and mental The assessor may, with your relative's permission, consult the doctor at the hospital, or your relative's GP, health visitor or community nurse for more information.

11

Medicines Does your relative need to take medicines regularly, and does this cause any problems?

Lifestyle, abilities, culture, ethnic background and personal factors such as bereavement How do these affect your relative's view of their situation and their ability to cope?

Whether there is a carer A carer has a right to be consulted as well, and, if they wish, to have their own needs assessed.

Who else is around to help Friends, neighbours, other family members, etc.

What help they are getting already From social services or other agencies.

Their housing situation Does your relative want to stay where they are? If so, does the house need to be adapted in any way? Or are they considering moving into retirement housing or a care home?

Transport Does your relative have difficulty in getting to the shops, doctor, etc?

Whether they are at risk Do they suffer from an illness which might cause them to collapse suddenly, for example diabetes, epilepsy or heart failure? Have they had a number of falls or other accidents or 'near misses' at home? Do they perhaps put themselves or others at risk by strange, threatening or erratic behaviour? (Sometimes people with Alzheimer's disease or short-term memory loss turn on the gas and then forget to light it – a risk both to themselves and to neighbours.)

Finance What income and savings does your relative have, and what benefits are they claiming? The assessor may ask for proof, such as pension books, or bank or building society statements. He or she may try to ensure that your relative is claiming all the benefits they are entitled to.

Your relative is entitled to ask to have the assessment in private, without you or another carer being present.

Each local authority has its own assessment procedure. You can find out how assessment works in your local authority by looking at a copy of its charter to improve services for people needing long-term support or care, which is called *Better Care, Higher Standards*. There should be copies at the social services department or at a Citizens Advice Bureau or perhaps at the local library or doctor's surgery.

You or your relative may feel that the assessment has not been carried out properly and that your relative has not had a chance to express their needs. Or you may feel that the services offered do not adequately meet the assessed needs, as discussed below. When the local authority gives you written advice of the outcome of the assessment, it must also give you or your relative information about how you can have the assessment reviewed. Your relative can also ask to be reassessed if they have serious doubts about the original assessment.

Meeting your relative's needs

Once your relative's needs have been assessed, the local authority has to decide about whether or not it will provide or arrange services. It makes these decisions by comparing your relative's assessed care needs with eligibility criteria which it has set for community care services.

If services are to be provided, then your relative should be given a written **care plan** setting out what services are being offered, what this is supposed to achieve and when their needs will be reviewed. Always ask to see the written care plan.

As well as the details of the agencies which will provide the services, the care plan should also contain the name and details of a contact to deal with problems. This may be the same person as your relative's **key worker**. (The worker in the social services department who is mainly responsible for looking after your relative's needs may be called their key worker.) The key worker or contact person should inform the local social services team if they become worried about your relative's condition and think that they need to be reassessed. However, if you feel that your relative's

13

condition has deteriorated and they should be reassessed, you can ask for this to be done. You don't have to wait for the key worker to ask for a reassessment.

If you feel that what the social services department is offering is inadequate to meet your relative's needs, you can make a complaint, using the complaints procedure, or ask for either a review or reassessment. Social services may, for example, offer to send someone in every morning to help them get up, but your relative may feel they can't manage without help in the evening as well.

Some of the services which could be offered if the social services department does decide to help your relative are listed on pages 18–21. This could include a temporary convalescent stay in a care home, as explained on page 17.

Although the services may be organised by the social services department, they may not be provided by them. Some may be provided by private agencies, or by voluntary organisations such as Crossroads or Age Concern. The social services department should contact all the different people involved in providing services for your relative.

Local authorities also have the power to give people money (called **direct payments**) to buy their own community care services once they have been assessed as needing help. It is now compulsory for local authorities to offer direct payments to older people who meet the necessary criteria. Your relative must use this money to organise and buy the care they have been assessed as needing. Carers can now also receive direct payments.

Sophie

Sophie's mother was admitted to hospital when she collapsed with heart failure. After about a fortnight she was ready to go home. But there was no one to look after her apart from her husband, also in his 80s. Although he was very willing, he didn't seem to have what it takes to be a full-time carer.

'Dad is a bit forgetful, he often falls asleep during the afternoon, and I don't think he has ever cooked a meal in his life. Fortunately social services were very understanding – I think maybe more than if it had been the other way round, and it was Mum caring for Dad.

'At first I was worried that nothing seemed to be happening. The social worker at the hospital seemed to be so busy, it was hard to get to talk to her. We didn't even realise Mum had been assessed – it just seemed as though they had come round for a chat. In fact the services have been excellent. When we hear what other people have had to put up with, we realise how lucky we've been.

'There were problems about Mum going home. She couldn't manage the stairs, and there was no bathroom or toilet downstairs. The occupational therapist from the hospital had been round before Mum was discharged, to talk about the arrangements and make sure she would be able to manage. Now the social services occupational therapist came round and recommended they had a stairlift put in. She said they could get a grant towards the cost.

'In the meantime, social services arranged for someone to come in the morning and give her a wash, and help her get dressed. And someone else comes in the evening and helps her get to bed. There is also a home help twice a week – the service is run by Age Concern on contract to the council. She has to pay a flat fee for the personal care, and the home help is charged at an hourly rate, but they are both very reasonable. Someone from another voluntary organisation comes and sits with her for an hour in the afternoon, and she also has a voluntary visitor from Age Concern.

'The community nurse has sorted out a wheelchair for her, so we can take her for walks round the block. And the occupational therapist came with a special raised toilet seat, and a frame round the toilet that bolts to the floor, so she can pull herself up.

'Mum and Dad can have meals on wheels, provided by a private firm on contract to the council, but she prefers the food my sister and I cook, so we stock up the freezer for them. Dad usually defrosts something for lunch.

'Mum gets the full Attendance Allowance, and all of it goes on paying for the carers who come in and look after her. Which is how it should be.

'At first they were a bit overwhelmed at having so many different people coming round all the time – especially my Dad. But they've got used to it now. Mum has got very fond of her carers.'

Making interim arrangements

If your relative really wants to stay at home but cannot cope on their own immediately, temporary arrangements may be necessary for the first few weeks.

Intermediate care

Intermediate care services are short-term care services which can be provided at home or in a care home and can involve both health and social services. They are intended to prevent people from having to go into hospital or remain in hospital unnecessarily. They are normally limited to a maximum of six weeks with the intention that, wherever possible, the support provided maximises the person's independence, so that they can live at home. The services available may include:

■ rapid response teams;
■ hospital at home;
■ residential rehabilitation;
■ day rehabilitation; or
■ supported discharge.

If an intermediate care package is offered to your relative, the health and social care services included in the package are provided free of charge. Intermediate care must involve active therapy, treatment or opportunity for recovery. It cannot therefore be used when simply waiting for a care home place to be available or for home care services to be put into place so that your relative can go home.

Other options for temporary care

Your relative may be offered care in a care home for two or three weeks as part of their 'care package'. If they have savings of £19,500 or less (in England in 2003, £20,000 in Wales, and £18,500 in Scotland where different rules apply), the local authority should contribute towards the cost of care (see pages 78–79 for more about paying for care in a care home).

If your relative is not offered care of this sort and you feel they need it, you can ask the local authority to provide it. If this is still refused, you could consider whether either you or your relative could afford to pay for care yourselves. A couple of weeks being looked after in a care home could make all the difference to your relative's ability to manage on their own in the long term, with the help of whatever support services you have arranged. Trying to manage on their own too soon could even mean that the arrangements break down and your relative ends up feeling that they cannot manage at home and going into a care home permanently.

If your relative does spend a couple of weeks in a care home, you may still find that you, or other carers, need to spend a week or so with them when they come out, as the transition from having everything done for them to managing alone may be too abrupt. Or you may feel that an overnight stay with them when they come out, with very frequent visits for the next couple of weeks, is a better way to ease the transition.

If the local authority does not offer free intermediate care or rehabilitation, and you feel you can't afford to pay for it yourselves, or your relative hates the idea of going into a care home even temporarily, you will need to consider other short-term options. These could include:

■ Your relative comes to stay with you (or another family member) for a few weeks.

17

- You (or another family member) stay with them for a few weeks.
- You and another family member (or members) take it in turns to look after them.
- You employ someone from a private agency to live in and look after them for a few weeks. The United Kingdom Home Care Association (address on page 114) can give you information about organisations that provide home care in your area.

Reassessing the situation

Whatever arrangements you make, you cannot be sure that things will work out exactly as you have planned. You and another family member may arrange to look after your relative alternative weeks for four weeks in all. Both you and your relative may feel sure they will be able to manage alone after this. But they may not recover as quickly as you all expected, or their condition could get worse rather than better. You would then have to rethink the situation completely. Making a long-term decision about your relative's future is the subject of Chapter 5.

Checklist of support services at home

Help with your daily routine	Contact
Help with housework, shopping, cleaning	*Social services, voluntary organisation or private agency*
Help with getting up, getting washed and dressed, going to the toilet, eating, getting undressed, going to bed	*Social services or voluntary care attendant scheme (eg Crossroads) or private agency*
Help with continence or continence supplies, eg pads, pants, bedding, etc	*Community nurse or continence adviser (ask the GP)*
Help with nursing, bathing, toileting, lifting	*Community nurse (ask the GP) or private nursing agency*

Laundry service	*Social services (in some areas only) or private laundry service (look in the* Yellow Pages*)*
Help with meals	**Contact**
Meals on wheels	*Social services or voluntary organisations (eg WRVS – Women's Royal Voluntary Service)*
Lunch club	*Social services, local community group, church or voluntary group*
Help with medical problems	**Contact**
Advice about most general health problems	*Your relative's GP who may refer them to someone else*
Nursing care at home, eg injections, changing dressings, etc	*Community nurse (ask the GP) or private nursing agency*
Advice about lifting or turning someone heavy	*Community nurse or physiotherapist (ask the GP)*
Advice on mobility and exercise	*Physiotherapist (ask the GP)*
Foot care, help with nail cutting	*NHS chiropodist (ask the GP or community nurse) or private chiropodist*
Help with aids, equipment and home adaptations	**Contact**
Advice on equipment to help with everyday living, eg washing, cooking, using the toilet, etc	*Occupational therapist (social services department or hospital) or disabled living centre (contact the Disabled Living Centres Council)*
Equipment for bedroom, eg rails, hoist, etc	*Community nurse or occupational therapist (social services)*
Mobility aids, eg wheelchair, walking sticks, walking frames, etc	*GP, physiotherapist, hospital (ask the GP) or Disabled Living Foundation*

19

Short-term hire of equipment	_British Red Cross (ask at the local branch), local Age Concern group, the WRVS or other organisations_
Adaptations to make your home more suitable for a disabled person	_Occupational therapist (social services department), housing or environmental health department, or voluntary organisation (eg home improvement agencies)_

Help with getting about	**Contact**
Help with transport	_Dial-a-ride or other voluntary organisation, social services or private taxi_
Transport to and from voluntary lunch club, day centre, etc	_Social services or community group_
Transport to shops	_Community or voluntary group. Some large stores run a bus service_
Advice about getting a specially adapted car	_Motability_
Parking badge (blue badge)	_Social services_
Disabled Person's Railcard	_Local railway station_

Social activities	**Contact**
Day centre, lunch or social club	_Social services, voluntary organisation (eg local Age Concern or Alzheimer's Society group) or community centre_
Holidays	_Social services or voluntary group (eg Carers UK), Holiday Care Service_

A break for the carer (respite care)	**Contact**
Someone to sit with your relative while you go out for a few hours	_Social services, voluntary organisation (eg Crossroads) or private agency_

Day care for your relative in a centre; may include lunch, social activities, use of bathing facilities, chiropody, hairdressing, etc	*Social services, hospital or voluntary organisation (eg Age Concern or Alzheimer's Society)*
Short-term care away from home, from a day to a fortnight. Could be in a hospital, care home, or even with another family	*Social services, hospital, care home*

For more *i*nformation

i Age Concern Factsheets (see page 120 for details of how to obtain factsheets):

6 *Finding Help at Home*

20 *Continuing NHS Health Care, 'Free' Nursing Care and Intermediate Care*

24 *Direct Payments from Social Services*

32 *Disability and Ageing: Your Rights to Social Services*

37 *Hospital Discharge Arrangements*

41 *Local Authority Assessment for Community Care Services*

46 *Paying for Care and Support at Home.*

Adapting the home

It is worth taking a good look at your relative's home and seeing if there are any changes which could make it safer or more convenient to live in.

Apart from general repairs and improvements, such as installing damp-proofing and insulation, you could make alterations to make the house more suited to the needs of an older or disabled person by adding:

- ramps leading up to doors with steps;
- a stronger stair rail;
- grab-rails by doors, and in the bathroom and toilet;
- wider doorways, to allow for a wheelchair;
- extra heating, or more convenient heating;
- a downstairs toilet and/or bathroom:
- a walk-in shower; or
- a stairlift or other internal lift.

You could also consider an **emergency response alarm system** (often called community alarms). Find out whether there is a council-run scheme in your area. If not, you might consider buying an alarm for your relative. Most alarms are operated by telephone, pull cord or by a pendant worn round the neck; or a combination of these. It means that if your relative does have a fall, they can call for help. The Disabled Living Foundation (address on page 109) has a factsheet called *Choosing a Personal Alarm System* and Age Concern locally may have information about what is available in your relative's area.

For further suggestions about simple things you can do to make the home safer, see pages 55–56.

Getting advice

If your relative has a disability, the best person to advise about any alterations to their home is an **occupational therapist (OT)**. OTs are trained to look at how people with disabilities can manage everyday tasks, such as getting about, washing, using the toilet, cooking, preparing drinks, eating, etc, and to suggest ways these could be made easier. OTs will advise about 'aids' – gadgets or equipment, such as special taps for people who have difficulty with normal ones, or magnifiers for partially sighted people – as well as about actual alterations to the home. OTs can be based either in a hospital or in the social services department of the local council.

You may find that there is a long wait for this service. In some areas, home improvement agencies (which are sometimes called Care and Repair or Staying Put) have been set up specially to advise older people and people with disabilities about repairing and adapting their homes. To find out whether there is one near where your relative lives, look in the telephone directory, ask the local housing department or Age Concern, or contact the national office, which is called **foundations** (address on page 109).

Assistance from the local authority

The local council might be able to help with adapting, improving or repairing your relative's home. Help can include providing a grant, a loan, materials or other forms of assistance. The council has to have a published policy setting out the type of assistance it will provide and in what circumstances. A summary of the policy must be available to the public on request.

Disabled facilities grants are available to provide facilities and adaptations to help a disabled person to live as independently and in as much comfort as possible. They are mandatory in specific circumstances. A grant must be given if a person is disabled and does not have access to their home and to the basic amenities within it, provided that they qualify on income grounds. This might include installing ramps for access to the house or installing a stairlift or providing a downstairs bathroom, for example. The local authority also has to agree that the work is reasonable and that it is possible to carry it out.

Local authorities can also give discretionary assistance for adaptations or to help someone to move to alternative accommodation. It may be paid in addition or as an alternative to the grant.

Disabled facilities grants are available from the housing department of the local authority but you can approach the social services department first as it has to be consulted about what adaptations are 'necessary and appropriate'. This will normally mean that you will receive a visit from an occupational therapist from social services. There can be lengthy delays, so apply as soon as possible.

You should *never* start the work before getting the council's approval to go ahead, or you will not be entitled to a grant.

To be eligible you have to be an owner-occupier, a private tenant (including a local authority or a housing association tenant) or a landlord applying on behalf of the disabled person.

Social services departments provide funding for some types of adaptation works, usually more minor adaptations such as grab-rails or bath seats which do not require structural work. They may also be able to help with the cost of work not covered by disabled facilities grants but the amount of help available varies between councils.

If your relative cannot get a grant and they own their own home, they could consider the possibility of raising some money on the value of the property, as explained in the publications listed below.

For more *i*nformation

ⓘ Age Concern Factsheets (see page 120 for details of how to obtain factsheets):

13 *Older Home Owners: Financial Help with Repairs and Adaptations*

35 *Rights for Council and Housing Association Tenants*

36 *Private Tenants' Right*

12 *Raising Income or Capital From Your Home.*

ⓘ *Using Your Home as Capital*, published annually by Age Concern Books (details on page 118).

ⓘ Carers UK information booklet *Getting Help to Adapt Your Home* (address on page 107).

3 Getting help and support

If you are already feeling anxious and under pressure, nothing is more likely to reduce you to complete desperation than not knowing who to contact about your relative – making one phone call only to be referred somewhere else, phoning the new number and perhaps being referred on yet again. This chapter aims to help you contact the right person, and to unravel the overlapping roles and responsibilities of the many different people who may be involved with the care of your relative.

*The two key places where you may find help with arranging care for your relative are the **GP's surgery** and the **social services department** of your local council. The GP is responsible for your relative's medical treatment. He or she is the person who will arrange the hospital and community-based health care. The social services department is responsible for organising services such as home care/home help and meals on wheels. Another key person is the **community nurse** (called the district nurse in some areas). The GP or someone from social services may ask the community nurse to call if your relative needs nursing at home.*

Penny

When Penny's father was diagnosed as having leukaemia he was told he had only a 20 per cent chance of surviving chemotherapy. The consultant haematologist at the hospital seemed brusque and unapproachable. It was hard to get information about the treatment, and how to cope with the after-effects of chemotherapy.

'When the chemotherapy was finished, he was transferred to a general ward, and by now Mum was feeling very anxious and depressed. She didn't know who to turn to. Dad was withdrawn, and, as the chemotherapy went on, became increasingly rambling and confused.

'Then Mum heard about CancerBACUP, the cancer charity. They gave her a lot of information, and suggested questions she could ask the consultant. They also put her in touch with the local Leukaemia Care Society, who had informative leaflets, and a whole network of local contacts Mum could turn to.

'They also told her about the Macmillan nurses. But when she asked whether she could get counselling, the consultant was opposed to it. I think he didn't really understand what counselling was about. He thought it was for people who were preparing to die.'

Fortunately, they had a sympathetic GP, who arranged for Penny's father to be seen by a psychogeriatrician.

'He confirmed that Dad's confusion was due to the chemotherapy. This seemed to change the consultant's attitude. Mum did get to see the Macmillan nurse counsellor, and found her very helpful.

'The nurse put Mum in touch with Carers UK, who helped them to apply for Attendance Allowance. She also put them on to the local hospice, where Dad was able to attend the day centre and have regular physiotherapy. This was a lifeline for Mum.'

Who's who in social services

The key department of your local council for people needing care is the social services department (called the social work department in Scotland). The social services department is responsible for coordinating the assessment of what care a person needs, and all the different care services if they decide to offer help (see pages 9–14). The person from social services who is responsible for your relative should liaise with the GP, the community nurse, and, if necessary, the hospital.

Understanding your local council

You may find yourself having to deal with various departments of the council, especially social services and housing. Local councils (also called local authorities) are organised differently according to where you live.

Big cities are usually **metropolitan boroughs** (or **metropolitan districts**), such as Tameside or Rotherham. All the services in the city come under the control of the borough (or district) council. London is divided into a number of **London boroughs**, such as Haringey or Sutton, which are responsible for all the services in that area.

In other areas, the local council covers a whole **county**, such as Devon or Lincolnshire. The county is usually divided into **districts**. The county is responsible for some services, such as social services, and the district for others, such as housing. In some areas unitary authorities have taken the place of counties, such as North West Somerset which was formerly part of Avon County Council, or Hartlepool which was formerly part of Cleveland County Council. All this can be very confusing. If you are not sure, look in your telephone directory. The local Age Concern or Citizens Advice Bureau will also be able to tell you how to contact social services.

In Scotland, all local authorities are unitary and a single local council has responsibility for all local authority services; for example Highland Council or South Lanarkshire Council. In Wales too, all local authorities are unitary; for example Caerphilly County Borough Council or Cardiff County Council.

Most social services departments have a head office and a number of divisions, such as elderly care services. Within each division there may be two or three smaller teams covering local communities. It will usually be the local team (for example East Team or West Team) which arranges care services for your relative.

Another important member of the team is the **occupational therapist** (OT), as explained on page 22.

If you don't know who to contact

Things are done differently in different parts of the country, so don't worry if you don't understand exactly how the local council is organised. The important thing is to be able to contact the right person to get the care your relative needs. If you seem to be getting nowhere, the local Age Concern group or carers' group may be able to advise you.

If the council is involved in your relative's care, ask for the name of your relative's key worker (see page 13) and for their direct line. In an emergency, if you do not know who to contact, ring up the local council and ask for the duty officer. There should be a **duty officer** (usually a social worker) available at any time of day or night, and they will advise you what to do, or pass your details on to the right person. If you cannot get hold of anyone who can help you, dial 999 and ask for the police.

Who's who in the health service

Many older people who need care and help at home have health problems and medical needs as well. In recent years government policy, including the National Service Framework for Older People, has aimed to make it easier for the health services and social services to work together.

There have been changes to the structure and organisation of the NHS bodies which deliver and plan healthcare. **Primary Care Trusts (PCTs)** have taken over from health authorities in arranging and commissioning services such as GPs, dentistry, community nurses and NHS hospitals (also called trusts). PCTs are local clusters of GP practices. In Wales bodies called **Local Health Boards** are responsible for the planning and provision of health services. In some areas in England new **Care Trusts** are being set up which will commission and provide both NHS and social care services.

Your relative's PCT area may be different from their local authority area – they often have different boundaries. You can find out which is their PCT by asking their GP or Citizens Advice Bureau. In every PCT there is a **Patient Advice and Liaison Service (PALS)** which is the first point of contact for patients and relatives. The PALS should be able to provide information on local services and support groups. NHS Direct (Tel: 0845 46 47) can tell you how to contact the PALS.

The PALS will also be able to tell you about a new service supporting those making a complaint – **Independent Complaints Advocacy Services** (ICAS), which have replaced Community Health Councils. These provide an advocacy service for people who want to make a formal complaint.

The National Health Service provides both community-based and hospital-based health services.

Community-based health services

When someone is ill, their first contact with the health service is usually at the GP's surgery or the local clinic or health centre. Apart from the GP, you may also be able to be put in touch with a **practice nurse**, a **health visitor**, a **community nurse** (sometimes called a district nurse) or a **community mental health nurse**.

The GP is the key person who can put patients in touch with all the other health services. He or she may ask the community nurse, health visitor or community mental health nurse to call on patients who need care in their own homes. The GP may also decide to refer them to the local social services department or to a hospital consultant if they need specialist medical care.

Social workers should liaise with the community-based health services, to make sure that people get all the help they need.

If someone needs hospital treatment they are usually referred to a consultant by their GP. But in an emergency you can, of course, dial 999 for an ambulance, or just go along to the casualty department.

Community-based health services

Professional	What they do
General practitioner (GP)	*Your family doctor, who can put patients in touch with a range of health services*
Community nurse	*Helps with practical nursing, eg bathing, lifting, turning, toileting, giving injections, changing dressings, etc. Can show you how to do these where appropriate*
Health visitor	*Visits families, usually with young children; sometimes visits elderly people and advises about other services*
Community mental health nurse (CMHN)	*Visits and advises people with mental health problems and their carers*
Interpreter	*Helps people whose mother tongue is not English (by translating during crucial interviews, etc)*
Continence adviser	*Offers advice, help and information about incontinence, including practical aids (pads, pants, etc). Ask the community nurse or GP to ask them to call*
Chiropodist	*There are often eligibility criteria for NHS patients (ask the GP or community nurse)*
Dentist	*Some dentists will visit at home (ask your local dentist or contact the local PALS)*

Optician	*Some opticians make home visits (ask your local optician or contact the local PALS)*
Community pharmacist	*Can answer questions about medication and give advice on common complaints*

Hospital-based health services

Doctors

A patient who comes into hospital is put under the care of a **consultant**, who is a specialist doctor. These are some hospital specialists you may come across:

Cardiologist Heart disease specialist.

Geriatrician Specialises in treating older people.

Neurologist Treats diseases of the brain and nervous system.

Oncologist Cancer specialist.

Ophthalmologist Specialises in eye problems.

Orthopaedic surgeon Treats injuries and diseases of the bones by surgery.

Psychiatrist Treats people with mental health problems and may prescribe medication.

Psychogeriatrician Specialises in mental illnesses in older people, including dementia.

Psychotherapist Treats people who are anxious or depressed or who have mental health problems, but does not prescribe medication.

Rheumatologist Specialises in diseases of muscles and joints, such as rheumatism and arthritis.

Urologist Treats disorders of the bladder and urinary tract, including prostate problems.

Under the consultant are a number of other doctors who are less experienced, but still fully qualified. These may be **senior registrars** or **registrars**, or they may be **junior doctors** or **house**

officers. They are usually responsible for the day-to-day treatment of patients.

Nurses

Nurses decide on nursing care and provide care and support for the patient.

The nurse with overall responsibility for the running of the ward is the **sister** or **charge nurse** or **ward manager**. Below the sister is the **staff nurse**, who will be a State Registered Nurse or Registered General Nurse, and State Enrolled Nurses. In some hospitals one **named nurse** has overall responsibility for the patient and will know most about the patient's nursing care. There may also be **student nurses, nursing auxiliaries, nursing assistants**, and **health care support workers**, none of whom are fully qualified nurses.

Some nurses are hospital-based, but can also visit at home to provide specialist care – for example:

Breast care nurse Specialises in caring for women who have breast cancer.

Diabetes specialist nurse Supports people with diabetes who require special care.

Macmillan nurse Provides support and advice for people with cancer and their families.

Stoma nurse Specialises in caring for people who have had an ileostomy, urostomy or colostomy.

Others

Other hospital-based professionals who sometimes visit at home include:

Occupational therapist Helps patients manage everyday tasks, and advises on any equipment for the home that may be needed.

Speech and language therapist Helps with communication difficulties and also with eating and swallowing difficulties, often working with people who have had a stroke or who have dementia.

Physiotherapist Helps people who have pain or difficulty in moving, using exercises, massage, manipulation, ultrasound, and other physical treatments.

Dietician Draws up special diets for patients to help them control their illness, and advises patients accordingly.

Dealing with 'the system'

Sometimes finding the right help is not easy, and you may feel frustrated and angry at all the delays and red tape. These hints may help you in dealing with social services staff or health care staff:

Remember, you are important As a caring relative or friend you are important to your relative's well-being. In fact, your support and love may be more important to them than all the other services put together.

But your relative's views are paramount You may, for example, think that your relative should have a private room in a hospital given their age and condition, but if they say that they are happy on a ward, then their view is more important than yours.

Be well prepared Before you talk to social services or health care staff, make a list of all the points you want to mention. Then tick them off as you go along. Make a note of what they say.

Be polite but firm You may find it helps to have someone with you for moral support when you meet with social services or health care staff.

See the professional's point of view If you are feeling upset or angry it can be hard to listen properly to what the other person is saying. Remember that they are only human too. It may help if you can show you are sympathetic to their position. ('I know you're under a lot of pressure ...' 'I really appreciate what you've done so far ...' 'I know you want the best for my mother/father/uncle/aunt but ...')

Keep names and phone numbers Make a list of the names and phone numbers of all the people you deal with, and note down what they do. You may want to flag up the names of people who were particularly helpful.

Keep a record of dates Record the date when you spoke to someone, and make a note of when they said something would happen. Then you can chase them up if it doesn't materialise.

Don't be afraid to complain If you are not happy with the way you are treated, don't be afraid to complain. All social services departments have a complaints procedure, which they are obliged to tell clients about. Just ring up the main number and say you want to make a complaint and you should be given the name of someone to contact. This person should also tell you how to contact someone to help you put your point of view (often called an 'advocate') if you need it. If you want to complain about health services, it is best to contact the PALS (see page 29) for further advice on how to do this.

Where to go for information and advice

Help needed	Where to go
Information about your relative's illness or disability	_There may be a relevant voluntary group or charity which can give advice and information (see address list at the back of the book)_
Information about benefits	_Citizens Advice Bureau, local social security office or local advice centre (and see pages 86–92)_
Information about what services are available for your relative	_The social services department of the area where your relative lives (see checklist of support services on pages 18–21) or the GP_
Advice and information about adapting your relative's home	_The occupational therapist at the social services department or a home improvement agency (see pages 22–23)_

Advice about most general health problems	*The GP*
Nursing care or advice about mobility, lifting or turning someone heavy	*Community nurse*
Advice about incontinence	*Continence adviser (ask the GP or community nurse)*
Information about making a Will or other legal matters	*Citizens Advice Bureau, law centre or solicitor (and see pages 94–95)*
Someone to talk to about your own problems	*Contact your own GP who may refer you to the community mental health nurse or to a counsellor or therapist (NHS or private)*
Support in bereavement	*CRUSE or Lesbian and Gay Bereavement Project (see addresses on pages 108 and 110). Hospitals, hospices and churches may also offer support*
Contact with other carers	*Ask the social worker if there is a carers' group, or contact the local Council for Voluntary Service or Carers UK (address on page 107)*
If you feel desperate	*Contact the Samaritans on 08457 90 90 90 or see your local telephone directory*

In an emergency, if you don't know who to contact or can't get hold of them, dial 999 and ask for an ambulance if it is a health emergency, the police for any other emergency or describe the situation to the 999 operator.

4 Common health crises in older people

This chapter looks at some of the health problems that are most common in older people and that may require emergency treatment and create a crisis situation for the family. It looks at dementia (including Alzheimer's disease), heart attack, stroke, cancer, and injury as a result of a fall. Some of the medical terms and treatments you may come across are explained.

Although dementia develops gradually over a number of years, it is included here because it is so often a crisis – an accident at home, a sudden illness, or the person suddenly wandering away and getting lost – which alerts the family to the need to take action. Cancer, too, develops gradually, but there may be points in the course of the disease when a crisis occurs; for example when it is first diagnosed and immediate treatment is necessary, or in the final stages.

For more detailed information, you are advised to go to one of the organisations or charities which specialise in that particular illness. These are listed at the end of each section.

Roy

Roy realised his father was getting a bit absent-minded and strange in his ways, but he didn't think anything of it until one night he was woken up by a knock on the door. It was the police. They had Roy's father in the back of the car. He was in his pyjamas and dressing gown.

'They'd picked Dad up wandering along the edge of the motorway. He said he'd lost his way. We were horrified to realise the danger he'd been in.

'We'd always thought he was quite happy living on his own. My wife or I dropped by every day. And he had good neighbours, who kept an eye on him after my mother died. They did tell us that he would occasionally knock on their door late at night, but they always made him a cup of tea and sent him home. This time they were away, and we think he must have set out to try and find us. Thank goodness the police picked him up before anything happened.

'We realised he wouldn't be able to live on his own any longer, but we really had no idea what to do. We put him to bed in our room and my wife and I bedded down on the sofa-bed downstairs. We didn't get much sleep. We spent the whole night talking about what to do.

'The police told us to contact social services, and they sent somebody round next day. They said it would be best if he went to live in a care home. Dad was very upset at the idea. He said we were locking him away. But after he'd been to see the home he perked up a bit. He likes company, and there were plenty of people to talk to. There's someone on duty at night if he feels like taking a midnight wander.'

Dementia

What is it?

The dementias are a group of diseases in which the brain progressively degenerates. **Alzheimer's disease** is a common cause;

another is **multi-infarct dementia**. It is estimated that one in five people over the age of 80 suffer from dementia.

People with dementia gradually lose their mental faculties and become confused. They tend to forget things that have happened quite recently, but may seem to have a clear memory of things that happened a long time ago. Their personality may also change. They may do or say strange and inappropriate things. They may wander about restlessly, especially at night. They may become angry and aggressive towards the person who cares for them, or they may become childlike and dependent. They may forget where they have put things, and accuse others of stealing them. They may forget to eat or to wash themselves, and they may put themselves and others at risk, for example by turning on the gas and forgetting to light it or forgetting that they have put food in the oven. All this can be very difficult and stressful for the carer, especially if the person is someone they have loved for many years.

A few early onset (before 60 years old) cases of Alzheimer's disease may have a genetic cause, but in the vast majority of cases the cause is unknown, despite continuing research efforts, although research continues to shed light on links and causes. If you have a relative or relatives with Alzheimer's disease and are worried that it might be 'in your family', you can ask your GP for a genetic test. Several factors are thought to predispose people to develop multi-infarct dementia, including smoking, overuse of alcohol, uncorrected high blood pressure and poorly controlled diabetes.

Not all confusion in older people is due to dementia. If your relative suddenly becomes confused or seems to lose their memory, they should see a doctor, as the confusion could be due to a physical illness or medicines they are taking. For example, some sleeping tablets can have the side effect of causing confusion. It is important that your relative's confusion is investigated and that they get a proper diagnosis.

What is the outlook?

Alzheimer's disease and multi-infarct dementia are progressive illnesses. That means that sufferers get gradually worse, and eventually die. How long someone will live depends a lot on their general health, and the age at which they develop the disease. Your GP or the hospital consultant are the best people to talk to about how the disease will affect your relative.

Some people with dementia manage to live in their own homes for quite a long time, with support from their family, social services and community health teams. After a while, however, it may be too risky for them to live on their own. It often happens that a sudden crisis, such as an illness or an accident, makes us aware that they can no longer cope alone.

At this point, a decision has to be made whether they will live with a family member or go into a care home (see pages 70–79).

Caring for someone with dementia

Caring for someone with dementia can be very stressful; it is not something that everybody can take on. If you decide this is the right option for you, then you will find it helpful to have as much information as possible about your relative's condition (see pages 6–7). You should also find out what support you can get through social services (see pages 18–21).

How you can help your relative

■ Help your relative's memory by having familiar objects and photographs around. Encourage them to keep a diary and to write things down. Keep a clock on view, and refer to the day and time when you talk. Establish a regular routine.

■ Make sure that your relative's physical health is looked after, and that eyesight and hearing problems are diagnosed and dealt with, as these can add to confusion.

■ Encourage self-esteem and independence. Treat your relative as an adult, help them to be clean and tidy, and encourage them to do as much as they can for themselves, or to do simple tasks around the house.

■ Avoid clashes, confrontations and arguments. It is better to change the subject, or distract them, than to get into a head-on row. But don't go along with muddled thinking or delusions. There may often be some basis in reality to your relative's delusions – for example, their neighbour may not be lying in wait to kill them as they assert, but he may have been unkind or rude in the past. Try to validate the reality and assert the rest.

■ Be very careful about safety in the home, especially where cooking, fires and gas are concerned. A person with dementia may be particularly prone to forgetting that they have turned an appliance on, or to turning on the gas and forgetting to light it.

Taking good care of yourself

Caring for a person with dementia is both physically tiring and emotionally stressful. Your relative may often keep you awake at night, or they may suddenly turn on you for no apparent reason, or they may forget who you are. As a carer, you will need plenty of help and support.

These DOs and DON'Ts may help:

Do look after your own health. See your own GP about health problems, and don't be afraid to mention psychological or emotional problems.

Do find out about respite care, so that you can have a break from time to time (see pages 20–21).

Do make contact with other carers. They could be your lifeline. You can find out about carers' groups in your area through the social services department, the local Age Concern group, Carers UK or the Alzheimer's Society (addresses on pages 107 and 105).

Don't be afraid to ask for the help you need, from social services, your doctor or your family.

Don't think you have to go on caring forever. As your relative's dementia progresses, you may feel that a care home is the only solution.

Don't feel guilty about it if you do make this decision.

For more *i*nformation

❶ The Alzheimer's Society (address on page 105) produces a number of useful books and leaflets. They will also put you in touch with other people in your area, so that you can share problems and information. In Scotland, contact **Alzheimer Scotland – Action on Dementia** (address on page 105).

❶ *Caring for someone with dementia*, published by Age Concern Books (details on page 116).

Heart attack

What is it?

A heart attack happens when the blood supply to part of the heart is suddenly blocked by a blood clot. It is more likely to happen if the **arteries** (the blood vessels which take blood to the body) are unhealthily clogged with a fatty substance called **atheroma**. Atheroma restricts the free circulation of the blood and encourages blood clots to form. A blood clot which blocks the artery where the clot is formed is called a **thrombus**, while one which is carried in the bloodstream from a different part of the body is called an **embolus**. Both are very dangerous.

The arteries which carry blood to the heart are called **coronary arteries**. If a thrombus forms in one of these, it is called a **coronary thrombosis**, which is another name for a heart attack.

If the arteries are badly clogged up with atheroma, a severe chest pain called **angina** is sometimes felt. This is a warning that a heart attack could happen, so if this pain occurs you should see the doctor at once. However, some heart attacks happen without any warning.

In a heart attack, the part of the heart where the blood has been cut off is damaged. The pain can be very intense, affecting not just the chest but sometimes the neck, jaw and inner arm as well. Some older people may have little or no pain. They may instead become faint, fall, have an attack of vomiting or become confused.

Smoking, high blood pressure, diabetes or unusually high levels of fat (**cholesterol**) in the blood are all factors which contribute to a build-up of atheroma and make a heart attack more likely.

Mina

'It came as such a shock when my husband had a heart attack. He was only 62, and he'd always seemed so fit and well, even if he did smoke a little bit more than he ought. He'd been complaining about pains in his chest a few days before, but I didn't think anything of it. I thought it was indigestion. Then suddenly he just crumpled up with this terrible pain in his chest. I phoned the ambulance, and fortunately they were pretty quick.

'They got him into hospital, and wired him up to all sorts of hi-tech machines. He looked so pitiful lying there with wires stuck all over him. What amazed me was the way they had him out of bed and walking about after a few days. I thought it was a bit cruel, but apparently that's what they do nowadays.

'At first, I was just relieved he was still alive. And with all the fuss and attention he was getting, we didn't really think about the future. Then they moved him off the special cardiac ward on to the general ward. He was with a lot of old men – at least, they seemed old – and he started to get depressed and anxious. "I don't look as old as them do I, Mina?" he'd say. Of course I reassured him, but the truth was, my view of him had changed. I'd always thought of him as the strong one in our relationship. Now I was seeing the vulnerable side of him.

'When he came home, it was even harder. He would swing between being optimistic and full of plans, and being down in the dumps. The doctor told me I should encourage him to do things for himself, not wait on him hand and foot. He said it was important to build up his independence. But I felt so mean.

'The best thing was, the doctor also told him he had to stop smoking and start regular exercise. He recommended walking. We started going out into the countryside during the week, when there was no one else around. Sometimes we would set out early and stop for a pub lunch. We discovered lovely places we'd never known about. And it brought us close together again. We were like a young couple, walking through the fields holding hands.

'Yes, the heart attack has changed our lives, but it's had some good effects, too. Jay is not as caught up in his work as he used to be; he realises there are other things in life.'

What is the outlook?

The outlook for someone who has had a heart attack depends on how severe it was and how soon they can get to hospital. The first couple of hours are absolutely critical, since this is when someone is most at risk of dying. If they survive for 24 hours, their chances of recovery are good. If there are no complications they may be sent home after about ten days, and will need to rest for another two or three months. Regular gentle exercise combined with drug treatment can help prevent another heart attack. Changes of lifestyle, such as stopping smoking in particular and taking a sensible diet, may also be crucial.

If one of the arteries is so badly narrowed that angina pains do not respond to treatment, surgery may be necessary. **Angioplasty** uses a hollow needle to insert a special small balloon into the artery. The balloon is then inflated, widening the artery, so that blood can flow more easily. **Coronary artery bypass** surgery involves grafting a vein from another part of the body to bypass the part of the artery which is blocked. Another treatment is **thrombolysis**, which seeks to dissolve a clot before the heart muscle is irreversibly damaged. For best results this has to be done soon after the clot forms.

43

Caring for someone who has had a heart attack

A heart attack is a great shock, not just physically but also emotionally. It may leave someone feeling depressed and anxious for several months.

There are several ways in which you can help your relative if they have had a heart attack:

■ Help them give up smoking. If you smoke yourself, and are living with someone who has had a heart attack, it will help them to give up if you stop smoking too – you will no longer be forcing your relative to breathe in your cigarette smoke and giving up smoking will also reduce your own risk of heart attack and cancer.

■ Help them lose weight if they need to. The doctor will tell them what their ideal weight should be, and will suggest a calorie-reducing diet if necessary. The doctor may suggest that the main thing to cut down on is fats – especially animal fats found in red meat, butter, cheese, eggs and non-skimmed milk – as it is thought that these can help cause the build-up of cholesterol in the blood which leads to atheroma.

■ Help them to exercise regularly. It is important to stick to an exercise routine recommended by the doctor, to build up fitness gradually, and not to overdo it.

■ Monitor and note any changes and, if you are worried, report them to the GP as they may be side effects of medication.

■ Emphasise the positive; many people who have survived heart attacks have happy and productive lives afterwards.

Heart failure

Heart failure is different from a heart attack. Heart failure means your heart does not pump enough blood to meet all the needs of your body. Usually this is because the heart muscle has been damaged, for example by a heart attack. Some of the other causes include high blood pressure, damaged heart valves, disease of the heart muscle due to genetic causes or damage to the heart muscle from a viral infection or from long-term heavy alcohol consumption.

Shortness of breath is the most common symptom. Weight gain and ankle swelling may occur. If your relative has these symptoms, their doctor may suspect heart failure and arrange tests to see if they do have it and, if so, how best to treat it. Heart failure is usually treated with tablets (called diuretics) to reduce the amount of fluid in the body and lower blood pressure, combined with different types of drugs. Sometimes other treatments will also be used, such as pacemakers, defibrillators and surgery.

For more *i*nformation

i **The British Heart Foundation** (address on page 106) has booklets about different kinds of heart disease, and recovery from a heart attack.

i *Caring for someone with a heart problem*, published by Age Concern Books (details on page 116).

Stroke

What is it?

A stroke is a type of brain injury. A stroke occurs when arteries supplying blood to the brain either get blocked or burst. The patient can no longer perform the functions the dead bit of the brain used to control.

Every stroke has different effects, depending on which part of the brain is damaged, and how severely. The most common effect is partial paralysis and loss of feeling on one side of the body – the opposite side to the part of the brain which is damaged. Mental ability, speech, vision and even personality can be affected.

Sometimes stroke signs appear but rapidly get better. This happens when the brain's blood supply is briefly cut off but is then restored. This is called a **transient ischaemic attack** or **TIA**. A TIA comes on suddenly and lasts for less than 24 hours; usually between 5 and 30 minutes. People who think that they may have experienced a TIA should see the doctor, as a TIA may be a warning of a more serious stroke or a heart attack.

Strokes are more common in people who have high blood pressure, heart disease or diabetes or who have recently had a TIA. Smoking, being overweight, taking little exercise and drinking too much alcohol all add to the risk. Although a stroke can occur at any age, 90 per cent of people who have a stroke are over 55.

Emily

Emily's mother was fit and active until she had a stroke, which left her paralysed down one side and unable to use her right arm. She then came to live with Emily and her family. She stayed with them for the next 20 years.

'She had always been a very active woman, and I knew I had to keep her busy and cheerful. She would still knit and iron with one hand. If I was cooking something, I would pass her the spoon and say, "Stir this for me, Mum."'

'I think the grandchildren kept her going. They behaved as though there was nothing different about her. We all tried to keep her cheerful and optimistic – I think that's very important. I was lucky to have a car, and we have a caravan by the seaside. If she was feeling miserable I'd say, "Would you like some fish and chips?" and we'd go off somewhere for a treat.'

Emily's mother has recently died, and Emily is left with a feeling of emptiness.

'We were tied for all those years she lived with us. I thought I would appreciate the freedom, but I find I miss her a lot. It's a strange feeling, suddenly having so much time on my hands.'

What is the outlook?

It is the extent and location of the stroke and the general health of the person at the time of the stroke that determines how well someone is likely to recover. Some people experience mild effects which improve in a short time, whereas others still suffer severe effects which last for months or years. Much recovery takes place spontaneously, but constant encouragement and the appropriate support of therapists will be important too.

A physiotherapist can advise about exercises to get a person moving again, and a speech and language therapist will help if speech has been affected. It is important to start exercising as soon as possible so that stiffness and loss of movement do not set in and become permanent.

Caring for someone who has had a stroke

If your relative has had a stroke, you can help by making sure that they do the exercises recommended by the physiotherapist and encouraging a positive attitude. Help them to get out and about, and make sure that they take any medicines that have been prescribed which will reduce the risk of a second stroke.

For more *i*nformation

ⓘ **The Stroke Association** (address on page 114) has information about caring for a stroke patient, and can tell you about local stroke clubs where you can get help and advice.

ⓘ *Caring for someone who has had a stroke*, published by Age Concern Books (details on page 117).

*C*ancer

What is it?

Cancer is not a single disease but a term covering over two hundred diseases in which some cells in the body start to multiply uncontrollably, and the cells form a lump called a **tumour**. Not all tumours are caused by cancer. Lumps in tissue may form for many other reasons. A cancerous tumour is described as **malignant**; a non-cancerous tumour is described as **benign**.

Cancer can happen anywhere in the body, but common sites are the lungs, bowel and prostate in men, and the breasts, lungs, bowel, cervix, uterus and ovaries in women. Other common cancers are **leukaemia** (cancer of the blood and bone marrow) and **lymphomas** (cancers of the lymph glands in many sites in the body, such as the neck, armpits and groin).

When a tumour grows to a certain size it begins to shed some of its cancerous cells. These are carried around the body in the bloodstream or the lymph system, and settle in other sites where they cause new cancers to grow. These secondary cancers are called **metastases**.

Some cancers are linked to chemical substances, such as asbestos, coal tar or tobacco (cigarette) smoke. In other cancers, particularly cancers of the reproductive organs, hormones are thought to play a part. Radiation is known to cause cancer. Even radiation from the sun – in other words, sunshine – can cause skin cancer. Some cancers are thought to be caused by a virus. It has been estimated that up to 35 per cent of cancers may be linked to diet, particularly tumours of the digestive tract, the breast and the prostate gland. A diet rich in fruit and vegetables is believed to help protect against these and other cancers.

Peggy

Peggy's husband Bill went to the doctor with a slight irritating cough that had been bothering him for a while. The doctor sent him to the hospital for an X-ray, and within four days the family were told that he had lung cancer.

'They told us he had a tumour as big as a grapefruit on his left lung. I was devastated. Bill put his arm round me and said, "We've been together for 45 years, and we'll get through this." Really, it was him that gave me strength.

'We were referred to the hospital, and after that everything seemed to happen very quickly. They took away his whole lung and some of the surrounding tissues. He had the operation on his 70th birthday.

'They kept him in a couple of weeks, and when he was allowed home, the community nurse came in every day to change his dressing. It was a huge cut, but it healed very well. Gradually he picked up, and we carried on. He couldn't play golf anymore because he couldn't swing the golf club, but he still went round the course with his friends, and he still went fishing. We went on holiday as usual in July.

'Then he started to get these pains across his shoulder. Our hearts sank when they told us he would need further treatment and would have to go to Weston Park. That's a specialist cancer hospital. We thought it was the end of the road. But everyone was so kind and friendly. It was a lovely atmosphere – not like a hospital at all. Even now, I would never be afraid of going into that hospital.

'He could still drive, so they let him come every day for his radiotherapy. We even went abroad on holiday that year, though he had to rest every afternoon.

'Then it spread down to his liver and tummy. He was sick a lot, and I was often up all night with him. He began to lose more weight, and he was very poorly. But he never lost his inner strength. However ill he'd been in the night, if someone came to see him next day, he always had a smile for them.

'At the end, it all happened very quickly. One day, he was still able to walk down to the bottom of the garden. That night, he was very ill. They asked him if he would prefer to go into hospital, but he wanted to stay at home, though he did agree to go into the hospice. But in the end it wasn't necessary. They offered us other help, too. We could have had a night nurse, and a special cancer care Macmillan nurse. But he didn't live long enough. We had two doctors from the local practice and two nurses popping in and out all the time. They put a needle in his hand, and there was a little pump which gave him a constant supply of painkiller, so he didn't suffer. We were all with him – the whole family. The vicar came and said a service round his bed. It was all so peaceful, just the way he would have wanted it to be.

'Although I was terribly upset, I think it happened the best way. We had four wonderful years after his first operation. Every day was a bonus.'

What is the outlook?

Cancer is by no means the dreaded incurable disease it was years ago. Many types of cancer that were incurable 20 years ago are now completely treatable. But it is still the second main cause of death in Britain (after heart disease). All cancers are different, and the doctor or specialist is the best person to advise you about the outlook for your relative. Older people who remember how cancer used to be may be unduly pessimistic. Many people who are diagnosed as having cancer will live to die of an unrelated cause.

Caring for someone with cancer

Even when you are told that your relative has not long to live, there is still much you can do to make their last weeks or months comfortable and happy:

- Offer small frequent meals, and plenty of drinks.
- If their mouth is dry and sore, offer cool drinks. The doctor may be able to prescribe something that helps.
- Help prevent pressure sores by moving or turning them regularly. The community nurse will show you how to do this.
- Take care of their skin with moisturiser or body oils, but avoid skin which has been damaged by radiotherapy. A gentle massage can be soothing and comforting. Be aware that in some people, even if they do not have skin cancer, the skin may be too sensitive to tolerate anything except water, and the body may be too sensitive to tolerate anything perfumed.
- Give painkillers regularly, rather than waiting until pain is severe. The doctor or nurse will tell you how much to give.

■ Help prevent constipation by adding a little roughage to the diet, such as a teaspoonful of bran, or fresh fruit and vegetables. People on strong painkillers may need laxatives, but do not give them to your relative without first seeking medical advice. If your relative has bowel or stomach cancer, it may be very unwise to alter their diet without seeking medical advice.

■ If continence is a problem, ask the GP or community nurse about supplies and advice. They can also tell you whether there is a laundry service in your area.

■ A radio by the bed, or a television with remote control, can help while away sleepless hours.

■ Show your love, by sitting with your relative and talking to them, or just holding their hand and letting them talk to you about their worries and fears.

Other sources of help

Macmillan nurses are nurses specially trained to look after cancer patients and their families. They give both practical advice and emotional support. Their knowledge and experience are much valued by the people they work with. You can contact a Macmillan nurse through your doctor or hospital, or through Macmillan Cancer Relief (see below).

Sometimes, when a person cannot get the nursing care they need at home, they may be offered a place in a **hospice**. This is a special hospital for terminally ill patients, where the staff are highly skilled in pain relief, and at dealing with the emotional side of terminal illness. (Some hospices also provide respite care.) Some hospices have an outreach team to treat people in their own homes; find out more about these from the Hospice Information Service (address on page 110).

For more *i*nformation

i **Macmillan Cancer Relief** (address on page 110) can give you information about how to contact a Macmillan nurse in your area.

i **CancerBACUP** (address on page 107) has a freephone information service and a range of useful publications.

51

ℹ *Caring for someone with cancer*, published by Age Concern Books (details on page 116).

Falls and fractures

Elderly people are particularly at risk of accidents and injuries at home – especially falls. Each year over 300,000 pensioners are so seriously injured by a fall in their home that they require hospital treatment.

Usually falls just cause bruising and superficial cuts – though even these can cause problems for frail elderly people. But the greatest risk is of fractures. Older people are especially at risk of fractures of the forearm and fractures of the hip. Hip fractures are more serious, because they can affect a person's mobility, and thus their ability to go on living independently, even after the fracture has healed. Crush fractures of the vertebrae are a cause of severe back pain, disability and deformity.

Anyone can have a fall, but some people are more at risk than others. These include:

■ people who are confused or mentally ill;
■ blind or partially sighted people;
■ people who have had a stroke;
■ people with chronic arthritis, Parkinson's disease, or other illnesses which can affect posture and stability;
■ people with poor co-ordination or reflexes;
■ people who are taking certain medicines, especially those with a sedative effect or which lower the blood pressure;
■ people who have been drinking alcohol;
■ people with some sorts of heart disease;
■ post-menopausal women; and
■ people who have had a previous fall.

Older women who fall are more at risk of fracturing a bone. This is because after the menopause women's bones may become more fragile through osteoporosis. Men can develop this too as they age, but much more slowly and less severely than women do.

Ray

Ray's mother lives on her own. Last winter, she fell on the front doorstep and banged her head. Fortunately someone saw her and called an ambulance and she was taken to hospital. They did a very thorough check, and gave her an X-ray. They couldn't find anything wrong with her, so they put her in an ambulance and sent her home.

'At about six o'clock that night, I got a phone call from mother. She sounded terrible, but she couldn't explain what was wrong. She said she couldn't make a cup of tea.

'Well, I live a hundred miles away, but I couldn't think of anyone to contact. So I jumped in my car and drove up. When I got there, she was still sitting in the same chair where the ambulance people had left her, and she had wet herself. She had simply been too weak to move. She was terribly distressed and embarrassed, as she had never been incontinent before. I cleaned her up and made her a meal and a hot drink. Then I put her to bed.

'Fortunately next day she was feeling much better, and she could get out of bed and potter around. I knew I would have to go back to work, so I spent the morning making a few phone calls and I organised a rota of people who would call in and make sure she was alright.

'The accident really made me aware of how vulnerable old people are living on their own, and I tried to persuade her to move into a sheltered bungalow or flat, where there would be someone to pop in regularly and make sure she is alright. The trouble is, she has lived in her house for 30 years, and doesn't really want to move.

'So, as a compromise, I got someone from the council to come round and check the house out for us, and I also got some leaflets from ROSPA (the Royal Society for the Prevention of Accidents). Fortunately I'm quite handy, so I've been able to make a few changes around the house – I've put a grab-rail in by the front doorstep where she tripped and I've put a stair-rail in, too. I've persuaded her to have a fitted carpet in the hall instead of a loose runner, and I've put an extra length of flex on the standard lamp, so it will go around the wall instead of across the floor.

'Now she's got her confidence back, she seems very cheerful. In fact, I'm the one who's worried. Before I left, I made sure I got the phone numbers of a few of her friends, her GP, the community nurse and the local social services. Now all I can do is keep my fingers crossed it won't happen again. But if it does, I'll be a bit better prepared.'

What happens after a fall

Someone who has had a fall, and is feeling bruised and shaken, may be taken to hospital for an X-ray, to make sure they have not fractured a bone. If there is no fracture, they will probably be sent straight home. Or if the GP is called, he or she may think there is no need for them to go to hospital.

If your relative has had a fall, it is important that they are not left alone, or sent home from hospital to an empty house. Even though they may seem to be alright at first, they will probably stiffen up and find it hard to move. They may find it hard to get to the toilet, or to make themselves something to eat or drink. Their confidence is also likely to have taken a knock, so they may not want to get up and move about. Or they may try to move, but be so stiff and shaky that they have another fall. For all these reasons, it is important that there is someone to keep an eye on them.

If you cannot stay with your relative, it is important to make sure that someone can at least pop in a couple of times a day to help them to the toilet if necessary, or make a meal or a drink for them. Sometimes it is hard to know who to contact, especially if it is the evening or weekend – see pages 4–6 for some suggestions.

Your relative may be sent straight home from hospital even if they do have a fracture. If they have a simple fracture, the limb may be put in plaster and they may then be sent home, or they may be kept in overnight for observation. Accident and Emergency units are used to treating injuries, but may not be aware of the other needs and problems of older people.

A serious or complicated fracture may call for a long stay in hospital. In older people, a fracture of the hip is most likely to cause complications, so a hip replacement is often recommended. If your relative is not able to move about and get some exercise during this time, their muscles may get so weak that it may be very difficult and painful to restore their ability to walk. For this reason, the hospital will try to get your relative up and moving as soon as possible. This usually means taking a few steps the day after the operation. Discharge arrangements should be anticipated as soon as possible, especially if home adaptations such as ramps and grab-rails are needed.

Before being discharged, patients should have their continuing health/social care needs assessed (see pages 9–14) and then be given a written care plan, which will relate to their community care on discharge. They should be asked to sign it to confirm that they agree to it. Social services have to check the adequacy of any care package provided within two weeks of discharge. An assessment of their ability to pay for community care services is also likely to be carried out. However, as a result of their assessment it may be decided that they are eligible for intermediate care (see page 16) or rehabilitation, in which case those services will be free.

Making the home safer

There are a lot of simple, straightforward things which can, if needed, be done to make the home safer:

- Remove all loose mats and rugs. Nail carpets down if possible.
- Make sure that stair carpets are properly fitted.
- Fit a strong rail at the side of the staircase. If your relative has had a stroke, and can only use one arm, fit a rail on each side.
- Use higher-wattage light bulbs in corridors and stairways.
- Do not use cupboards or shelves which are so high that you need to stand on a chair to reach them. Use them for storing things which are seldom used, or leave them empty.

- Install grab-rails by the bath or shower and toilet.
- Use non-slip mats in the bath or shower if it does not already have a special non-slip surface.
- Install grab-rails by the front and back steps, and by any internal steps.
- Tape trailing flexes around the edges of the wall. Try to avoid tucking them under carpets, as they can fray without anyone realising it, and cause fires.
- Use extra table lamps or side lamps to lighten dark corners. This can also mean that if the ceiling light bulb goes your relative will not have to change it themselves or wait in the dark until help arrives. (But make sure flexes do not trail across the floor.)
- If glass doors are not made of safety glass, cover them with a shatterproof film (from DIY shops).
- Have gas appliances and flues checked regularly. If possible, use gas installations with a flame supervision device/safety lid on the hob – this means the gas will be turned off automatically if it is not lit.
- Have electrical wiring checked by an electrician. Make sure that sockets and fuses are not overloaded.
- If there are open fires, make sure that there is a fireguard, and that it is easy to use.

If you or your relative can afford it, you could also consider getting fitted carpets which eliminate the risk of tripping on the edges of rugs and of slipping on rugs without a stable underlay, as well as being easy to keep clean. A microwave cooker may be easier to use, and may cut down the risk of burns on hot pans, provided that your relative is capable of understanding the instructions and is not at a stage, for example in dementia, where new equipment may cause confusion. A microwave is also more economical for cooking or heating up small quantities of food.

For more *i*nformation

i See pages 21–24 for further suggestions about ways to make the home safer and more convenient for an older or disabled person to live in.

i Age Concern Factsheet 37 *Hospital Discharge Arrangements* (see page 120 for details of how to obtain factsheets).

i Alzheimer's Society Advice Sheet 503 *Safety at Home* (address on page 105).

i **The Royal Society for the Prevention of Accidents** (RoSPA – address on page 114) produces books and leaflets about home safety.

5 Making a long-term decision

This chapter looks at the long-term decisions you and your relative may have to make about how they will be cared for. If they have been seriously ill or injured, they may no longer be able to manage living at home, even with care and support.

Before any decisions are made, your relative and other members of the family will want to talk through the options. If your relative lives with someone, the decisions will obviously affect them too. It is worth taking time to think about all the issues, and making sure that everyone is involved.

It is important to involve someone from social services, too, as they will be able to tell you what is realistically possible in the area where your relative lives, and what is not. A lot may also depend on how much money you and your relative have.

When talking through the options, it is worth bearing in mind that your relative's condition may well change and the decision you make may therefore not turn out to be a final one.

Rosemary

Rosemary's mother was very independent and capable until she was 91. Then she had a series of minor strokes which left her feeling confused and agitated. The doctor said she should no longer live on her own. Rosemary suggested she should come and stay on a temporary basis while they decided what to do.

'My brother and his wife came over from Manchester, and we all sat down and discussed what would be best. Our son was away at college, and our daughter had already decided she wanted to go and get a flat of her own with some friends. So although we only have a three-bedroom house, room was no problem. What's more my husband had just retired from his job, so he would be there to give me a hand. My brother and his wife were both still working full-time, but they could have her to stay from time to time to give us a break.

'Many people have no choice about caring for a relative, and I don't want to pass any judgements. But we did have the choice, and for us it just seemed the right thing to do.

'We did our best to make her feel at home, by bringing things from her house and putting them in her room. She had a Welsh dresser she was fond of, and we brought that and put it downstairs. In fact after she'd been with us a while she seemed to forget all about her own home.

'Mother did once go into a care home for a fortnight, while we had a holiday. But she wasn't happy there. It's not that they didn't look after her. On the contrary, perhaps they did too much for her, because we noticed there were things she'd been able to do for herself that she could no longer cope with.'

Rosemary has no regrets about the three years she spent caring for her mother.

'I'm not saying it was always a picnic. But we could see she was happy with us. Her friends would come and visit. The vicar used to drop in. We would all laugh and joke. It felt natural. Now that she's died, we all feel glad she was with us until the end. In fact it was a joy.'

What are the options?

Before coming to any decision, you and your relative and the rest of the family will want to look at all the possible options. Looking through the eight options for your relative listed below could be a good starting point, although the options listed are obviously not exhaustive.

1 They could **carry on living in their own home**, but with more help and support, and maybe some alterations to make their home more suitable.
2 They could **move into retirement (sheltered) housing** or some other kind of housing with support.
3 They could **share their house with a friend** or move in with a friend and they could support each other.
4 They could **move to live near you** or another family member.
5 You or another family member could **move to live near them**.
6 They could **move in with you** or another family member.
7 You or another family member could **move in with them**.
8 They could **move into a care home**.

In each case there are of course many different ways things could be organised, depending on your relative's individual circumstances.

The advantages and disadvantages of each option are discussed on pages 61–65.

Can your relative live independently?

The first thing for you and your relative to decide is whether they can live on their own (or with another person such as a spouse or friend), provided that they get enough help. Even if it seems that your relative will be able to go on living on their own, the situation may change if their condition becomes worse.

If you are in any doubt, ask the social services department to make an assessment of your relative's needs (see pages 9–14). You might find it helpful to talk to their GP or the community nurse or the consultant who looked after them if they have been in hospital.

Advantages and disadvantages of the different options

Option 1 *Your relative carries on living in their own home*

Advantages

- May be what your relative wishes.
- Independence and privacy may be retained.
- Familiar surroundings, which may help your relative to retain memories.
- Less upheaval.
- Friends and neighbours close by.

Possible disadvantages

- Risk of further illness or injury (your relative may be willing to accept some risk if they want to stay at home).
- Not enough help available.
- Loneliness (especially if your relative is housebound).
- Family possibly too far away to visit frequently.

Things to look into

- The long-term outlook for your relative's health.
- Support services at home (see pages 18–21).
- Adapting the home (see pages 21–24).

Option 2 *Your relative moves into retirement housing*

(Retirement housing is described on pages 66–70.)

Advantages

- Most of independence retained.
- Risks reduced if there is a residential manager or warden.
- Purpose-built housing: easy to look after, may be all on the same level.
- No need to make alterations to existing home.
- Possibly some communal facilities and activities.

Possible disadvantages

- Unfamiliar surroundings.

- Upheaval of moving.
- Nuisance of having to sell present home.
- Expense: depends on housing scheme, service charges, and whether buying or renting.
- Possible waiting list.
- May be available only in wrong area.

Things to look into

- Retirement housing schemes in the area (contact the council's housing department and the Elderly Accommodation Counsel – address on page 109).
- Support services at home (see pages 18–21).

Option 3 *Your relative shares their home with a friend (or shares friend's house)*

Advantages

- Mutual support and care, and company.
- Familiarity of friend, or of neighbourhood, or both.
- Shared costs.

Possible disadvantages

- Friendship may be placed under strain.
- Friends in the same age group may not be able to meet each other's age-related demands.
- May involve upheaval for one or both for an arrangement which is short term.

Things to look into

- Legal and financial considerations arising out of sharing a property.

Option 4 *Your relative moves to live near you*

Advantages

- Independence retained.
- Family close by.

Possible disadvantages

■ Unfamiliar surroundings/loss of reminders of personal history.
■ Upheaval of moving for what may be a short-term solution.
■ Loss of contact with friends and neighbours, which may increase dependence on you.
■ Difficulty of finding suitable place.
■ What happens if you have to move to a different area?

Things to look into

■ Retirement housing schemes in the area (contact the council's housing department and the Elderly Accommodation Counsel – address on page 109).
■ Support services at home (see pages 18–21).
■ Adapting the home (see pages 21–24).

Option 5 You move to live near your relative

Advantages

■ Most of independence retained.
■ Familiar surroundings.
■ Less upheaval.
■ Family and friends close by.

Possible disadvantages

■ Upheaval for you and your family for what may be a short-term solution.
■ Financial implications if you have to give up work.
■ You may lose contact with your own support network.
■ Difficulty of finding suitable place.

Things to look into

■ Housing and employment possibilities in the area you are thinking of moving to.
■ Support services at home (see pages 18–21).
■ Adapting the home (see pages 21–24).

Option 6 *Your relative moves in with you*

Advantages

- Less risk if someone is always or often there.
- Your relative may like to be cared for by their own family.
- Companionship for your relative.
- Sense of relief for you.

Possible disadvantages

- Loss of independence for your relative.
- Upheaval of moving.
- Stress for you and your family: you may feel that you have no life of your own and that you have lost your own independence.
- Possible friction and bad feeling between you and your relative.
- Your home may not be suitable.

Things to look into

- Support services at home (see pages 18–21).
- Adapting the home (see pages 21–24).
- Legal and financial considerations arising out of sharing a property.

Option 7 *You move in with your relative*

Advantages

- Familiar surroundings.
- Less upheaval for your relative.
- Friends and neighbours close by.
- Your relative may like to be looked after by their own family.

Possible disadvantages

- Loss of independence for you and your relative.
- Upheaval for you and your family.
- Stress for you and your family: you may feel you have no life of your own.
- Possible friction and bad feeling between you and your relative.
- Your relative's home may not be suitable.
- Financial implications if you have to give up work.

Things to look into

■ Support services at home (see pages 18–21).
■ Adapting the home (see pages 21–24).
■ Legal and financial considerations arising out of sharing a property.

Option 8 *Your relative moves into a care home*

(Care in care homes is described on pages 70–79.)

Advantages

■ Safety: someone is always there.
■ Round-the-clock care.
■ Good facilities.
■ Possible companionship.
■ Less disruption for you.

Possible disadvantages

■ Loss of independence and privacy.
■ Unfamiliar surroundings.
■ Loss of contact with family, friends, neighbours.
■ Your relative may feel unwanted and unloved.
■ Family may feel guilty.
■ Expense: if your relative has savings over £19,500 (in England in 2003, £20,000 in Wales, and £18,500 in Scotland where different rules apply), or social services do not think they *need* care in a care home, they may have to pay the full cost (see pages 78–79).
■ Difficulty of finding a place in a home that has the facilities for someone with your relative's disability.
■ Difficulty of finding a home your relative likes.

Things to look into

■ Care homes in suitable areas (contact the local social services department or the National Care Standards Commission or the Elderly Accommodation Counsel – addresses on page 111 and 109).

Talking things over

With so many different needs and views to take into account, talking through the options can be more difficult than you would think. It may help if you are aware of some of the possible sources of misunderstanding. You may then be able to smooth over disagreements, or present things in a different way which makes them easier to understand.

These are just some of the ways misunderstandings can arise:

■ Your relative, or other members of the family, may be confused and not really understand the options.

■ Your relative may want to avoid upsetting anyone, and this may lead them to say different things to different members of the family or go along with other people's suggestions.

■ Your relative may change their mind but not feel able to say so because they feel under pressure.

■ Your relative may resist some options because they feel that they are being rejected.

■ Different members of the family may have strong feelings about what should happen. Your relative may feel under pressure to agree to suggestions, even if the pressure is not deliberate.

■ Your relative may believe that they are going to die soon, so there is no point in making any arrangements. Or other members of the family may think this. But no one will voice this thought.

■ Different people may be given different information by health and social services staff.

■ People may feel torn between conflicting emotions such as love, guilt and resentment, other commitments, even financial considerations. There may be hidden resentments between family members.

Retirement housing

Retirement housing, which is also known as sheltered housing, is special housing for older people or people with disabilities who are fairly independent, but want the security of having someone there to keep an eye on them. Most retirement housing is in purpose-built developments of flats (and sometimes bungalows), which are rented from the local council or a housing association or sold on a leasehold basis. There is almost always an alarm system which is linked to a communications centre which can summon help in an emergency. Usually there is a resident manager or warden on site, but sometimes there is a mobile warden who keeps an eye on a number of retirement housing schemes.

Another advantage of retirement housing is that the units are quite small and easy to heat and look after. If it is important to your relative to be on the ground floor, then check that a bungalow or ground-floor flat is available.

The services provided in retirement housing can differ considerably from scheme to scheme. In some schemes, the manager or warden is there all the time, and may also arrange for shopping, home help/home care and other services. In other schemes, the warden just drops in daily or once in a while to check that residents are alright. All other arrangements have to be made individually by the residents.

Renting retirement housing

Demand for rented retirement housing is high. The best way to find out about council and housing association retirement housing in your relative's area is to contact the local council's housing department.

The main thing taken into account when a council or housing association considers applications is the person's housing need at the time they apply. The amount of time spent on a waiting list may be immaterial. Each application is considered on its merits.

Many housing associations allocate 50 per cent or even 100 per cent of their properties to people nominated by the local council. To nominate someone, the council must be satisfied that they are a 'high priority' for retirement housing.

Retirement housing to buy

Most retirement housing is sold on a leasehold basis. This means that your relative will have a long lease on the property and will usually pay a small ground rent to the freeholder. It is very important, if you are thinking of buying into one of these schemes, to find out exactly what is included in the purchase price, and what extras there are. You should check how much the service charge will be and what regular outgoings there will be, for example for heating, service charges, maintenance, cleaning, gardening, water rates, Council Tax, etc.

Abbeyfield houses

Abbeyfield houses cater for people looking for support in retirement housing. Most of the accommodation is in large houses with unfurnished bedsits for eight to twelve older people, and a resident housekeeper. The weekly charge usually includes two main meals a day and facilities for residents to prepare their own breakfast and snacks. A typical house also offers a call alarm system, an assisted bathroom and a network of support from local volunteers. You can get more information about schemes in your relative's area from the national address on page 105.

Retirement housing checklist

If your relative has decided that retirement housing is right for them, they will also want to consider which features will be important to them in choosing a particular scheme. As well as factors affecting any move, such as the location and the community and transport facilities locally, it will be useful to think about the following questions:

■ Is the alarm system linked to a 24-hour monitoring service? How reliable is the system and what action can your relative expect if they call for help?

■ What exactly are the manager's/warden's responsibilities? Do they meet your relative's needs? Are they medically trained/qualified?

■ Is the person on call on site? Is there relief cover when they are not on duty?

■ What arrangements can be made for other care services, such as home help/home care, visits from the community nurse or GP, meals on wheels, hairdressing, chiropody? Is there an additional fee for some services?

■ Is the flat/bungalow accessible? Does your relative need to be on the ground floor? Is it all on one level inside?

■ Is the flat/bungalow big enough? Is there room for your relative's furniture? Is there sufficient storage space?

■ What facilities are there in each flat/bungalow? If your relative is (or were to become) disabled, is the flat/bungalow suitable? Does it have any special adaptations, such as wide doors, wheelchair ramps, internal lifts, grab-rails by the entrance doors and in the bathroom and toilet, waist-level sockets, lever taps, easily opened windows, a walk-in shower?

■ Are there any communal facilities, such as a social room, TV lounge, laundry facilities, shared garden area?

■ Are there visitors' rooms, so friends and relatives can come to stay?

■ What are the other people who live there like? Do you think your relative will get on with them? Are there any organised social activities or outings? Is there an extra charge for these?

■ Does your relative understand/mind that the warden will have a set of keys and will be able to enter your relative's flat/bungalow?

■ Are pets allowed?

■ Is there a policy about smoking in communal areas?

■ Who runs the management organisation and how often do their representatives hold meetings with residents? Are they members of the Association of Retirement Housing Managers (ARHM)?

■ Is there a residents' association?

■ How much does it cost to live there? And what does the rent/service charge include? What about repairs, heating, water rates, Council Tax, TV licence? Are there any hidden extras you need to know about? When and how often do fees increase?

■ Are there circumstances in which your relative's lease can be terminated without their consent, for example if they became mentally ill or developed Alzheimer's disease? How secure is their tenancy?

For more *i*nformation

❶ Age Concern Factsheets (see page 120 for details of how to obtain factsheets):

2 *Buying Retirement Housing*

8 *Looking for Rented Housing*.

❶ **The Elderly Accommodation Counsel** (address on page 109) can provide lists of accommodation to rent or buy in all parts of the UK.

*C*are homes

For some people, moving into a care home might be the best answer. Making a decision about moving into a care home is never easy, because it is such a big step for anyone to admit they can no longer manage on their own. If you and your relative are not sure what level of personal or nursing care they need, this will be clarified for you when the social services department assesses your relative's needs (see pages 9–14).

Some homes have had rather a bad name, and many people are still reluctant to consider this alternative for their relatives. Nowadays homes are regulated by the National Care Standards Commission (which in 2004 will amalgamate with the Social Services Inspectorate to become the Commission for Social Care Inspection) and there are better complaints procedures.

When you are looking for a care home for your relative, one of your first ports of call is the local regional office of the Commission (national address on page 111). They can supply you with a list of homes in the area and you can also ask to see copies of the inspection reports of the homes in which you are interested. In some areas copies are also available in local libraries. If the reports do not answer your questions, you can telephone the regional office of the Commission and ask to talk to an inspector.

Some homes provide nursing care at all times (by having a registered nurse on duty 24 hours a day) and some provide personal care with any nursing needs of residents being met by visits from the community nurse. Some provide both kinds of care, possibly in different wings of the home. Some care homes will cater especially for people at various stages of dementia.

Mina

'Mum suffered from Parkinson's disease, and my father looked after her. When he telephoned to ask me to call the doctor, I knew something was very wrong. I jumped in my car and drove the 250 miles to where they lived. By the time I got there, the doctor had arrived, and he had called an ambulance. Dad had had a heart attack, and Mum was dehydrated and confused. The doctor arranged for them both to be admitted to hospital.

'After about a fortnight, the hospital started to pressure me to remove Mum. They said there wasn't anything more they could do for her. Dad was still in hospital, so I went down to fetch her. I put Mum and the cat in the car, and brought them up here. Mum was disorientated and confused. She wanted to go home. She just wanted things to be as they had been before.'

Mina arranged for her mother to see a geriatric consultant at the local hospital, where she was diagnosed as having Alzheimer's disease and admitted for three weeks while her medication was sorted out. But the weekend she was discharged, there was a phone call from the hospital saying Mina's father was seriously ill.

'We tried to find someone to look after Mum. The social services department couldn't help us – they told us to contact Crossroads. But before they could sort it out, Dad died. I'll always regret that I wasn't able to see him before he died.'

Mina found looking after her mother increasingly stressful. She thought about giving up her job, but decided against it because her husband's job was not secure. The children found their eccentric grandmother difficult to live with, too.

'It was a very hard time for the whole family. She couldn't be left on her own. She needed someone there all the time, in case she did anything dangerous. But then she always picked arguments. We'd never had an easy relationship, but now I was just finding it impossible. The whole family was under stress. In the end, it was the geriatric consultant who said she would be better off in a care home. He told us about a new home that had just opened. It wasn't perfect, but they were friendly and kind. Mother was delighted.'

At first Mina's mother seemed happy, but as her illness progressed she became listless and depressed, and wouldn't eat. After a year, the home could no longer cope. Mina would have to find a home that could give her mother more nursing care.

'We were given a list of homes, but none of them seemed suitable. One was upmarket, but the atmosphere was cold; another seemed shabby and crowded. I despaired of finding the right home and I got to the point where I thought I would have to take the next one with a vacancy whatever it was like, as the process was very tiring.

'Eventually I widened the area I was looking in and visited a home that was further away; one I had passed on my way from work that had looked nice from the outside. We went to visit, and we liked it at once. It had a good atmosphere, and they had a place. I was so relieved.

'When I visit Mum she seems much happier. Sometimes she tells me outrageous things, but then I realise she's confusing it with the boarding school she went to as a child. I do feel guilty sometimes – I feel I've sidestepped my responsibilities. But I also know that for us personally we had no choice.'

How social services can help

If the social services department assesses your relative and decides that they cannot manage in their own home, and need to be in a care home, they may arrange a place for them. This could be a council-run care home, a private home, or one run by a voluntary organisation or charity. If your relative's capital assets are £19,500 or below (in England in 2003, £20,000 in Wales, and £18,500 in Scotland where different rules apply), they will help toward funding the costs, as explained on pages 78–79.

If you want a different home to the one suggested by social services

Your relative can choose the home they wish to live in, so long as the owners of the home are prepared to make a contract with the council. But if the home costs more than the council usually pays, you may have to make up the difference. For more information about third party contributions, see Age Concern Factsheet 10 *Local Authority Charging Procedures for Care Homes*.

The council should not, however, set an arbitrary limit to what they are prepared to pay. They should pay the full cost of a place to meet your relative's assessed needs. If you are not satisfied with what the council offers – for example, you feel that your relative needs to be somewhere where their family can visit them easily and the council has offered a place 50 miles away, and your relative has been, or you believe they should have been, assessed as needing proximity to their family for social or mental health reasons – then you can argue that the cheaper home does not fully meet your relative's needs and make a complaint. All social services departments must have a complaints procedure.

Choosing the right home

It is not easy to choose a home for another person. The things which matter to your relative may not be the things which seem most important to you, so it is helpful if you can talk together about what you are looking for in a home. If your relative is severely mentally disabled, or confused and finds the decision too stressful to think about, this may not of course be possible, and you will have to make the decision on your own or with other members of the family.

If you have difficulty in finding a place in a home, you may feel so grateful when you do find one that you make the mistake of accepting the first one that is offered. If you cannot find a home that will accept your relative, you should talk to an inspector at the local office of the National Care Standards Commission (NCSC) You may also find it helpful to contact Counsel and Care or the Elderly Accommodation Counsel (addresses on pages 108 and 109). You should also speak to your relative's social worker if they have one.

If at all possible, it is a good idea to visit a number of homes – even if they don't have current vacancies – so that you can make comparisons, and be confident that the home you choose for your relative is right for them.

If the home is well run, they will not mind you asking a lot of questions. They will be pleased that you are concerned for your relative.

Care home checklist

Does the home meet your relative's needs?

- Does it take people with your relative's illness/disability?
- Does it provide the right level of care (for example nursing care if necessary)?
- Is it in a convenient place for you to visit regularly?
- If your relative is in a wheelchair, is there good wheelchair access to all parts of the building?
- Is the building all on one level, or is there an internal lift?
- If your relative needs special treatment or a special diet, will the home be able to provide it?

■ What will happen to your relative if their condition deteriorates or improves?

■ If your relative becomes very ill, will they be able to remain in the home or will they have to go into hospital or a hospice?

■ Is there a vacancy? How long is the waiting list?

■ Is it possible for your relative to stay in the home for a trial period of a week or two, to see whether it suits them?

Is the home well run?

■ Are there sufficient trained staff?

■ What staff are in the home at night?

■ Is the home properly insured?

■ Have you seen the most recent NCSC inspection reports?

■ Is the home secure enough for your relative if they 'wander'?

■ Is it clean? Is it homely? Are there plants and flowers around?

■ Are there any pets?

■ What is the food like? Is there a choice (as there should be)? How large are the portions?

■ How do the staff seem to behave towards the residents?

■ What happens if a resident has a complaint?

Does the home encourage residents to be independent?

■ Are residents encouraged to do things for themselves and make decisions for themselves as much as possible?

■ Can residents be involved in everyday activities such as cleaning, cooking, gardening, looking after pets?

■ Do residents usually look after their own money? What are the arrangements if they are not able to?

■ Does the home respect residents' need for privacy? Do staff knock before going into a resident's room?

■ Can residents prepare food and drinks in their own rooms?

■ Can residents see visitors when and where they choose?

■ Is there a telephone residents can use for incoming and outgoing calls where they can talk in privacy?

■ Can residents decide for themselves when to go to bed and when to get up in the mornings? If not, are you happy with the arrangements?

- What are the arrangements for handling medicines? Do residents have a say in this?
- Can residents see their own doctor, or is there one doctor who sees all the residents in the home?
- Does the home let residents have a say about how things are run? Is there a residents' committee? Is there a relatives' support group?
- Can you still be involved in helping your relative if you want to (and they want you to)?

What are the facilities like?

- Are the rooms single or shared? If your relative has to share a room, is there any choice about who they share with?
- Will your relative be able to reach a toilet easily, both from their own room and from the dining room and other shared areas?
- Is there more than one living room, so that there is a quiet room as well as a television room?
- What is the policy about smoking? Will this suit your relative? If your relative does not smoke, are there enough smoke-free areas?

Will your relative be happy there?

- Are the other residents the sort of people your relative could get on with and make friends with?
- Will your relative be able to keep any personal possessions in their room, such as pictures, plants, flowers, furniture?
- If your relative is physically active, will there be enough activities (apart from watching television) to keep them busy?
- Are there up-to-date books, newspapers and magazines for residents? Does a mobile library visit, or can residents go to the local library?
- Are there any organised activities residents can get involved in? Does the home take residents out on trips and visits, for example shopping, or to the theatre or cinema, or to a place of worship?
- If your relative likes gardening, is there any opportunity for them to be responsible for an area of garden?

How much will it cost?

- How much is the weekly fee? What exactly does it cover?
- What are the extras? Ask about hairdressing, chiropody, extra drinks or snacks, continence supplies, special diet, newspapers, a television or telephone in your relative's own room, trips and outings, treatments such as physiotherapy, speech therapy or massage (if relevant to your relative), and any other services you think your relative will need. Some items or services which are necessary as a result of your relative's condition may be provided through the NHS – ask the manager of the home, the GP or social services. (Residents or their visitors will usually be expected to buy things for personal use such as clothes, toiletries, stationery, etc.)
- Do you have to pay a deposit on booking? Is it refundable?
- If the home puts up its fees, how much notice will you get? Is this likely to happen annually? Will the increases take the fees beyond the amount the local authority is willing to pay (if your relative has a funded place)?
- If your relative is away from the home for a short time, for example in hospital or on holiday, what fees will they still have to pay?
- Is there a contract to sign? Who has to sign it – the person staying in the home, or another family member? (If you are asked to sign a contract on behalf of your relative, you should seek legal advice from a solicitor or Citizens Advice Bureau about what exactly you are committing yourself to.)
- How much notice will you have to give if your relative leaves the home?
- What happens about payment if your relative dies while they are in the home?

Balancing everybody's needs and wishes is never easy. Remember that there is no perfect solution. Whatever option you and your relative choose, there are bound to be times when you regret it and feel you have made the wrong decision. The important thing is to be happy in your own mind that you and your relative considered all the options and made the best decision in the circumstances.

Paying for care in a care home

Care homes can be very expensive, but if your relative's capital assets are £19,500 (in England in 2003, £20,000 in Wales, and £18,500 in Scotland where different rules apply) or below, they may get help with the cost. If, however, your relative goes into a care home temporarily to receive care support under the label of 'intermediate care' (see pages 16–17) or 'rehabilitation', they will not have to pay for it. The rules about paying for care in a care home are extremely complicated. They are explained in detail in the free Age Concern Factsheet 10 *Local Authority Charging Procedures for Care Homes*. The information below will give you a general idea of the position.

In England the NHS is now responsible for meeting the cost of registered nursing care for residents in care homes (but not for nursing care provided by a nursing assistant). For more details see Age Concern Factsheet 20 *Continuing NHS Health Care, 'Free' Nursing Care and Intermediate Care*.

In most circumstances, anyone who has savings or investments over £19,500 will have to pay the full cost of a place in a care home. However, the NHS fully funds the care of some people who have high levels of care needs (see Factsheet 20). Some people in England receive their care free under Section 117 of the Mental Health Act.

If your relative is funded by the local authority and owns a house or flat, its value could be counted as part of their savings. However, this does not apply if they are only going to be in a care home temporarily, or if their spouse or another 'relative' who is aged 60 or over or is disabled still lives there. The local authority has discretion to ignore the value of the home when someone else lives there.

Even if your relative starts by paying the full cost, they can apply to the council for help as their savings drop down to £19,500. Their eligibility for benefits should be assessed and the council should reassess your relative's means. Ask for an early financial assessment if your relative's savings will soon have been reduced to £19,500. It is possible to get Pension Credit (see page 91) even if they have quite a lot of capital as there are no upper capital limits.

For more *i*nformation

i Age Concern Factsheets (see page 120 for details of how to obtain fact-sheets):

10 *Local Authority Charging Procedures for Care Homes*

29 *Finding Care Home Accommodation*

20 *Continuing NHS Health Care, 'Free' Nursing Care and Intermediate Care*

38 *Treatment of the Former Home as Capital for People in Care Homes*

39 *Paying for Care in a Care Home if You Have a Partner*

40 *Transfer of Assets and Paying for Care in a Care Home.*

i **Counsel and Care** (address on page 108) is a voluntary organisation which gives advice and information about care homes. It may be able to help if you have difficulty in finding a place in a home.

i **The Relatives and Residents Association** (address on page 113) provides support and advice for the relatives of people who are in a care home.

6 Money matters

If your relative becomes very ill, physically or mentally, you may need to take steps to take over the running of their affairs. Even if your relative's illness is not too prolonged, you may well need to arrange to collect their pension and other benefits for them. If they are ill for a long time – or they are not likely to recover – you (or another family member) will probably need to take over the running of their affairs more completely. Obviously you will do this with your relative's consent if they are capable of understanding what they are doing; if they are not, you may have to take over without their consent. This chapter explains how you do this.

It also looks at some of the benefits that may be available either to your relative or to you as a carer, so that you can check that you and your relative are claiming any benefits you are entitled to.

Finally, this chapter explains why it is important to make a Will and how to go about making one. If your relative becomes very ill and has not made a Will, they may want you to help them make one – or you may want to try to persuade them that it is a good idea.

Maninder

Maninder's mother suffered from Parkinson's disease, and was cared for by her husband. She became increasingly confused after her husband died. Eventually she was diagnosed as having Alzheimer's disease, and the geriatric consultant said she should be in a nursing home. Maninder realised that she would now have to sell her parents' house.

'We contacted a solicitor, and he said something about Enduring Power of Attorney. But they messed us about for such a long time drawing up the document that by the time it was ready it was too late. Mum's confusion had returned, and she couldn't sign it. So we had to go through the whole business of obtaining the forms from the Court of Protection and getting a doctor to complete one of them certifying that she was mentally incapable, and could not make her own decisions. The forms then had to be returned to the Court and eventually a Receivership Order was issued, which enabled me to sell the house and handle her affairs. That took six months.

'The house was then placed with an estate agent, and fortunately it was sold quite quickly. The Court of Protection gave instructions as to where the money should be invested.

'I have to account for everything I spend on my mother's behalf. The first year was very difficult, when there were all sorts of small detailed expenses like the newspaper bill and the milkman to pay off. Now it's settled more into a routine. I have to keep records and receipts of all expenditure – her nursing home fees, the occasional shopping trip, Christmas and birthday presents, and so on.

'I wish I'd known earlier about Enduring Power of Attorney. Then we could have avoided all this.'

81

Taking over responsibility for someone's affairs

Collecting pension and other benefits

If your relative is still mentally capable – that is, able to understand what they are doing and what documents mean – they can nominate you or another relative to collect their State Pension and other benefits. There are a variety of ways of doing this.

Agent

If your relative receives a benefit or pension, they can nominate you as their 'agent' to collect the money for them, but not to spend it. An agency card can be obtained from the social security office stating that you, as the named person, are authorised to collect the money.

The Government is phasing in changes to the way that benefits and pensions are paid so that by 2005 most people will receive their money paid directly into a bank, building society or post office account. If you collect money on behalf of your relative, you will need to check how you can do this with the different types of accounts. If you are not sure which of the options are suitable, get further advice from a local agency. People will continue to be able to get their benefit or pension by order book at least until Autumn 2004 and even after then there will be some exceptions to the system.

Appointee

If your relative is not able to manage their money, you may be able to become their 'appointee' (you have to be in regular contact with them in order to qualify). As an appointee, you will be responsible for withdrawing money from your relative's pension on their behalf, but you will also have other responsibilities. It may be best to get some advice before taking on this role as there are administrative tasks involved.

For more *i*nformation

ℹ Social security leaflet GL 21 *A Helping Hand for Benefits? How Somebody with an Illness or Disability Can Get Help to Collect or Deal with Social Security Benefits.*

ℹ Age Concern Information Sheet LC/16 *Changes to Pension and Benefit Payments.*

Enduring Power of Attorney

In England and Wales, power of attorney is a document which gives someone the legal right to manage another person's affairs, for example if they are ill in hospital or away on holiday. An **ordinary power of attorney** only applies so long as the person giving it is mentally capable.

An Enduring Power of Attorney (EPA) is different from an ordinary power of attorney in that it remains valid even if the person giving it later becomes mentally incapable. But it must be created by someone who is mentally capable at the time.

This can be a good idea if your relative is getting more forgetful and absent-minded, and you think that they may soon become incapable of managing their affairs. You may be worried that they are beginning to suffer from dementia. This is not an easy subject to discuss with your relative, and for this reason many people avoid it until it is too late. If talking about creating an Enduring Power of Attorney causes such bad feeling that it could poison your relationship, it may be best to seek advice (from the GP, solicitor or Citizens Advice Bureau), or try to get a third party to help you explain to your relative how helpful an EPA might be if they become ill for example. Someone who is less involved might be better able to help your relative overcome their worries about making an EPA – an EPA can help enormously in overcoming a later stressful situation.

An EPA can allow you to take over your relative's affairs at once, if that is what your relative wants, and to continue handling their affairs if they become mentally incapable in the future, or it may appoint you to take over their affairs only if they become mentally incapable. Some people draw up an EPA that will come into effect only under certain conditions, such as their doctor diagnosing them as having dementia. You could discuss these conditions with your relative, and write them into the agreement. Sometimes people do this at the same time as making their Will, as a way of preparing for the future.

As soon as you believe that your relative is becoming or has become unable to manage their affairs or to supervise your actions, you *must* apply to the Public Guardianship Office (which carries out the administrative work of the Court of Protection) to have the EPA registered. Once it has been registered, you can show the document to the bank, building society, etc, if you want to withdraw money or carry out other transactions. (If the EPA permits you to take over your relative's affairs at once, you should do this immediately.) However, there are still rules about how you can spend the money.

You can buy a special document to create a power of attorney from a legal stationer, or you can ask a solicitor to draw one up for you. A useful booklet called *Enduring Power of Attorney* is available free from the Public Guardianship Office (address on page 113).

Applying to the Court of Protection

The Court of Protection is the body charged with a duty to provide financial protection services for persons who are not able to manage their own financial affairs because of mental incapacity. If your relative becomes mentally incapable of looking after their own affairs before they have given you an Enduring Power of Attorney, you may apply for help from the Court of Protection. In England and Wales the Court of Protection can appoint a '**receiver**' and in Northern Ireland the Office of Care and Protection can appoint a 'controller'(usually a relative, friend or solicitor), who can have authority to do anything that the person would do if they were still capable of acting for their own benefit. Different rules apply in Scotland (see below). Expenses incurred will come out of your relative's funds.

Applying to the Court of Protection is costly and complicated, so it is better to avoid it if you can by encouraging your relative to create an EPA in good time.

For more *i*nformation

i Age Concern Factsheet 22 *Legal Arrangements for Managing Financial Affairs* (see page 120 for details of how to obtain factsheets).

i **The Public Guardianship Office** (address on page 113) produces a number of free explanatory booklets and leaflets.

Managing someone else's affairs in Scotland

Under the *Adults with Incapacity (Scotland) Act 2000* a new Office of the Public Guardian (OPG) has been established which administers orders and appointments relating to adults with incapacity. Part 4 of the Act, 'Management of residents' finances', however, is regulated by The Scottish Commission for the Regulation of Care (The Care Commission).

Continuing Power of Attorney

The power which will allow you to act for your relative if they should become incapable is called a Continuing Power of Attorney in Scotland. It is signed by both parties – the grantor (your relative) and the attorney – and by a solicitor or GP. It is registered at the time it is made, not at the time your relative becomes incapable.

If there is no Continuing Power of Attorney in existence when your relative becomes incapable of acting for themselves, then you will have to apply to your local Sheriff Court for either financial guardianship or welfare guardianship or both.

For more *i*nformation

i Age Concern Scotland Factsheet 22S *Legal Arrangements for Managing Financial Affairs* (see page 120 for details of how to obtain factsheets).

ⓘ *Dementia: Money and Legal Matters*, a free leaflet from Alzheimer Scotland – Action on Dementia (see address on page 105).

ⓘ **The Office of the Public Guardian** (see address on page 112) can provide information about Continuing Power of Attorney and financial or welfare guardianship.

Benefits, pensions and tax

Being ill or disabled may prove very expensive for your relative, particularly if they have to pay for care. You, too, may find all kinds of unexpected claims on your budget, from paying someone to do the garden because you are too busy to do it to contributing towards the costs of care services for your relative. It is therefore worth making sure that both you and your relative are claiming any benefits you may be entitled to.

The benefits system is quite complicated, and claiming everything you are entitled to can be difficult and time-consuming. You do not have to be an expert to claim benefits, but it certainly helps to have some idea of what you are entitled to, and possibly someone who is an expert to advise you. The Citizens Advice Bureau or another local advice centre is a good place to start. There is also a Benefit Enquiry Line for people with disabilities on Freephone 0800 88 22 00.

This section also looks very briefly at pensions – it is always worth checking that your relative is claiming all the pensions that are due to them and that they are not paying more Income Tax than they should be.

Rosemary

When she was 91, after a series of minor strokes which left her feeling confused and agitated, Rosemary's mother came to live with Rosemary and her husband. Rosemary looked after her mother for the next three years, until she died. Rosemary has no regrets about caring for her mother, but she does feel angry that she was never told about the benefits her mother could claim.

'I found out about Attendance Allowance completely by chance from the girl in the village post office. We realised she could have been claiming it for two years, but nobody told us. It was the same with the Council Tax. A friend I met at church told me that elderly mentally disabled people didn't have to pay. Otherwise we would never have known.'

After her last stroke Rosemary's mother became much more confused, needing care during the night as well as during the day. They applied for the higher level of Attendance Allowance, which covers day and night-time care.

'We were told she would have to wait six months. I think that's very niggardly. If she needs care now, why should she have to wait six months to get the allowance?'

Hints on claiming benefits

- ■ If you are not sure whether there is a benefit you or your relative could claim, explain the situation and ask if there is help available.
- ■ If you think you or your relative could be entitled to a benefit but you are not sure, you can always claim anyway: you have nothing to lose.
- ■ Make your claim as soon as possible. Some benefits cannot be backdated before the date when you first claim.
- ■ If you or your relative have been refused a benefit you think you are entitled to, don't be afraid to appeal.
- ■ Get an 'expert' to help you make your claim or appeal.

Benefits for people with a disability

Attendance Allowance

This is a weekly allowance paid to people aged 65 or over who become ill or disabled and have care needs. It is meant to help with the costs of being ill or disabled, although it is up to the person how they actually spend the allowance.

To qualify for Attendance Allowance people must need help with personal care (washing, dressing, eating, going to the toilet, etc), supervision, or to have someone watching over them.

Attendance Allowance is paid at two rates. The lower rate is for people who need care either during the day or at night. The higher rate is for people who need care both during the day and at night.

A person must usually have been disabled for six months before they can get the allowance, but someone who has been diagnosed as terminally ill can be paid it straightaway.

Attendance Allowance does not depend on National Insurance contributions, nor is it affected by income or savings. People do not pay tax on it, and it does not affect other social security benefits.

Disability Living Allowance

Disability Living Allowance (DLA) is for people who become ill or disabled and make a claim before the age of 65. There is a 'care component', paid at three different levels according to how much looking after people need, and a 'mobility component', paid at two different levels according to how much difficulty they have in moving about.

Like Attendance Allowance, DLA does not depend on NI contributions and is not affected by income or savings. It is tax-free, and can be paid on top of other benefits.

Statutory Sick Pay (SSP)

SSP is paid by the employer instead of wages for up to 28 weeks to someone who is too sick or disabled to work.

Incapacity Benefit

This is a benefit for people who have been working but then are unable to work owing to illness or disability. It is based on NI contributions and is not means-tested, but a personal or occupational pension of more than a certain amount may reduce benefit. The long-term rate cannot be paid after pension age, so your relative should then draw the State Pension.

Industrial Injuries Disablement Benefit

This benefit compensates someone who has become disabled as a result of an accident at work or through contracting an industrial disease.

For more *i*nformation

𝒊 Age Concern Factsheet 34 *Attendance Allowance and Disability Living Allowance* (see page 120 for details of how to obtain factsheets).

𝒊 *Your Rights: A Guide to Money Benefits for Older People*, published annually by Age Concern Books (details on page 118).

Benefits for carers

Carer's Allowance

Carer's Allowance (which used to be called Invalid Care Allowance) is the only benefit specially for carers. It is for people who cannot work full-time because they are looking after someone who is severely disabled. You do not have to live together or be related. You may qualify for Carer's Allowance if you meet the following conditions:

■ You look after your relative for at least 35 hours a week (including evenings, nights and weekends).

■ You do not earn more than a certain amount (net of certain work expenses).

■ Your relative receives Attendance Allowance, the higher or middle levels of the care component of Disability Living Allowance, or Constant Attendance Allowance.

The benefit is not dependent on NI contributions. It is taxable. There is now no upper age limit for claiming, although if you are receiving a State Pension or another benefit you may not receive the allowance on top of this.

It is counted as income if you are getting a means-tested benefit such as Income Support, Pension Credit, Housing Benefit or Council Tax Benefit. But it may still be worth claiming, as it entitles you to the carer premium, paid with these benefits (see below).

If your relative receives the severe disability premium with Income Support, Council Tax Benefit or Housing Benefit, or since October 2003 the severe disability addition in Pension Credit, they will lose this if you claim Carer's Allowance for yourself. If in doubt, ask the Citizens Advice Bureau or another local advice agency to calculate whether it makes sense for you to claim.

The carer premium/addition

This is an extra amount of money paid to a carer as part of their Income Support (and Pension Credit), Housing Benefit or Council Tax Benefit. You will be entitled to the carer premium if you are entitled to Carer's Allowance (even if you don't get Carer's Allowance because you are already getting other benefits).

For more _i_nformation

ⓘ Social security leaflet SD 4 _Caring for Someone?_ describes benefits for carers and for disabled people.

ⓘ Carers UK Information Sheet _Benefits: What's Available and How to Get Them_ (address on page 107).

Benefits and other help for people with low incomes

Income Support

Income Support helps with basic living expenses by topping up people's weekly income to a level set by the Government. It is a benefit for people under 60 who don't need to be seeking work, for example because they are a carer. It is means-tested – which means that income and savings are taken into account. You can claim it if you have no more than £8,000 in savings, your income is below a certain amount and you work less than 16 hours a week.

Pension Credit

Pension Credit replaced Income Support in October 2003 for anyone aged 60 or over. Pension Credit also has a savings credit providing additional cash to people aged 65 and over with modest incomes. There is no upper savings limit.

Housing Benefit

Housing Benefit helps with the cost of rent for people on a low income. It is generally only awarded to people who have no more than £16,000 in savings, although the savings limit does not apply to some people receiving Pension Credit.

Council Tax Benefit

This benefit helps with the Council Tax (called rates in Northern Ireland) for people on a low income. As with Housing Benefit, it is generally only awarded to people who have no more than £16,000 in savings, although the savings limit does not apply to some people receiving Pension Credit.

The Social Fund

Makes lump-sum payments in the form of a grant or loan to help people on low incomes with exceptional expenses. **Cold Weather Payments** and **Funeral Payments** are mandatory (that is, they must be made if you fulfil the qualifying conditions), and **Community Care Grants**, **Budgeting Loans** and **Crisis Loans** are all discretionary. Budgeting Loans and Crisis Loans have to be paid back but they are interest-free.

Help with the Council Tax

In addition to Council Tax Benefit (see above), people may be helped with the Council Tax in various ways:

- If someone living with you (not your partner or a lodger) has a low income, you may qualify for 'second adult rebate', which functions like a discount off Council Tax.

- People living on their own get a discount of 25 per cent. Adults who are 'severely mentally impaired' and some carers are not counted as an extra person.
- People with disabilities may get a reduction if their house has certain special features.

Help with health costs

If you receive certain benefits you can get free prescriptions and sight tests (these are free to people aged 60 or over anyway), help towards glasses, hospital travel costs and dental treatment. If you have a low income and no more than £12,000 in savings (£8,000 if you are aged under 60), you may still be able to apply for some help by filling in form HC 1.

For more *i*nformation

ⓘ Age Concern Factsheets (see page 120 for details of how to obtain factsheets):

48 *Pension Credit*

25 *Income Support*

17 *Housing Benefit and Council Tax Benefit*

49 *Help From the Social Fund*

21 *The Council Tax and Older People*

5 *Dental Care and Older People.*

ⓘ Department of Health leaflet HC 11 *Are You Entitled to Help With Health Costs?* is available from post offices.

Pensions

As well as checking that you and your relative are claiming any benefits you may be entitled to, it is worth checking that your relative is collecting any pensions that are due to them.

State Pensions

Most people who have worked get a pension from the State when they reach State Pension age (currently 60 for women, 65 for men). The exact amount they get depends on how many National Insurance contributions they have paid during their working life. It is not affected by income or savings but it is taxable.

Your relative's State Pension may consist of a **Basic Pension** plus an **Additional Pension** (introduced in April 1978) and a **Graduated Pension** (based on contributions between April 1961 and April 1975). They will receive an extra 25p each week when they reach the age of 80.

Married women, widowed people and divorcees who do not qualify for a full Basic Pension may be able to claim a pension based on their spouse's contributions.

Occupational and personal pensions

Your relative can check for any old pensions that they may have forgotten about with the **Pension Schemes Registry** (address on page 112) which has details of thousands of schemes and can tell you how to make contact with any past scheme.

If your relative has a problem with an occupational or personal pension that they cannot sort out with their former employer or the pension provider, contact the **Pensions Advisory Service** (address on page 112).

Tax allowances

It is also worth checking that your relative is claiming all the tax allowances that they are entitled to. A tax allowance is the amount of income you are allowed to receive without paying any Income Tax. There are special tax allowances for people aged 65 and over, and for registered blind people. If you think that your relative may be entitled to an extra tax allowance, contact the local tax office (Inland Revenue).

For more *i*nformation

ℹ Age Concern Factsheets (see page 120 for details of how to obtain factsheets):

19 *The State Pension*

15 *Income Tax and Older People.*

ℹ *Your Taxes and Savings*, published annually by Age Concern Books (details on page 118).

Making a Will

Making a Will tends to be something that people put off, because they find it upsetting to think about death. If your relative has not made a Will, you may find raising the subject of making one extremely hard, especially if they have a terminal illness. But in fact it may put their mind at rest if they can talk about what will happen to their money and property when they die. You could ask, 'Have you thought about what you would like to do about ...?' You could even suggest making a Will yourself to make it all seem more everyday. You could ask other people who have been in the same position for advice about how to broach the subject tactfully.

People sometimes think it is not worth making a Will because they assume that anything they own will automatically go to those closest to them. But if your relative dies without making a Will, or the Will is not valid, or if they have got married or divorced since making the Will, there are strict rules laid down in law about how the **estate** (their money and property) will be divided. These rules can cause difficulties and sometimes hardship for families. It can mean that people your relative would like to provide for are not included.

A Will makes it easier for the relatives to carry out someone's wishes after they die. The Will names one or more people to be the **executors**: this means they will be responsible for sorting out the dead person's estate and carrying out the instructions in the Will. The executor is usually a surviving spouse or other close relative, but it could be a professional such as a solicitor or bank manager. A professional executor will usually charge a fee, which is paid out of the estate.

Getting help with making a Will

It is best to ask a solicitor to help with drawing up a Will, especially if your relative's financial or family situation is at all complicated. The fees solicitors charge can vary a great deal, so it may be worth ringing up a few solicitors and asking for a quotation. If there is a family solicitor who has looked after the family's affairs for a number of years, you may prefer to go to them.

Some people draw up their own Wills. It is important that the Will is clear, and that it is dated, signed and witnessed in the right way. Otherwise it will not be valid. The witnesses to the signature cannot be beneficiaries or their spouses; the executor can be a beneficiary.

Be careful if you are drawing up your own Will in Scotland. Many of the pre-printed forms available are designed for use outside Scotland where the rules are different.

For more *i*nformation

❶ Age Concern Factsheets (see page 120 for details of how to obtain factsheets). Scottish versions are also available:

7 *Making your Will*

43 *Obtaining and Paying for Legal Advice.*

❶ Age Concern also publishes a leaflet, *Instructions for My Next of Kin and Executors Upon My Death*, which can be left in a convenient place to tell the family where all your relative's important documents are, including their Will.

❶ *Make Your Own Will: Action Pack (England and Wales)*, *Wills and Probate* and *What to Do When Someone Dies*, all available from Which Ltd, Freepost, Hertford X, SG14 1SH. Freephone 0800 252100. (Prices on application.)

7 If the person you are looking after dies

If your relative dies while you are making strenuous efforts to care for them, this may come as a great shock. You may feel a rush of different emotions which are almost overwhelming: panic, grief, fear, loss, relief, guilt, anger, regret, loneliness, to name but a few.

If your relative dies in hospital, the staff will take care of the practicalities, and you may have some space to begin to come to term with your own feelings.

If you are with your relative at home as they approach death, you will probably be doing all you can to make them feel comfortable, and you may not have time to think about your own feelings until afterwards.

A feeling of panic often arises after someone has died because you feel you ought to be doing something, but you have no idea at all what you should do. This section gives you a step-by-step guide to all the practical things that need to be taken care of when someone dies.

Ann

'During the last two days when we knew my father was going to die very soon I felt sad, but I couldn't cry. I was with him when he died and I cried then but I remember the first overwhelming feeling was one of relief. It's as if you're in limbo when you know someone is going to die – there's absolutely nothing you can do but try and hold yourself together.

'Now, looking back, I think I think I just went numb, but I didn't realise it. I didn't really start to cry until three or four days after he died. My mother was in quite a state and I wasn't trying to be stoical but I think one part of my mind decided to just shut down until it was safe to let go. My mother went through a phase of being very angry – at everything – but I didn't feel that. Just terribly sad and empty.

'For about six months afterwards I felt very raw – I had no self-confidence – even small problems got on top of me. Unexpected things would start me crying – stories on the news about somebody dying, or a game of rugby on TV because he used to love rugby when he was younger. Gradually it got less painful when I thought about him.'

From *Caring for someone who is dying*, published by Age Concern Books

Things to do at once

1 Give yourself a little time

Before you do anything else, you may want to just sit down quietly and give yourself time to gather your thoughts. There is no 'right' or 'wrong' way to feel at this moment – people have very different reactions. Some people like to be alone with the dead person for a little while but others do not. Some people feel overwhelmed with feelings of sadness and grief, some feel drained of emotion, some feel dazed or numb. All these reactions are normal and natural.

2 Call the doctor

If the GP has been looking after your relative through their illness, and knows the cause of death, he or she will confirm that they have died, and issue a **medical certificate** giving the cause of death. You must give this to the registrar when you go to register the death (see point 7 below). The death must be registered within five days. The GP should also give you a **formal notice** stating that the medical certificate has been signed and explaining how to register the death.

If your relative is to be cremated, you will need an extra form signed by a different doctor. The funeral director or the GP will arrange this. The Will should be read to see if it contains any instructions about the funeral, and the executor should be consulted before any funeral arrangements are made.

Sometimes, if the doctor has not seen the person who has died in the last 14 days, or would like to know more about the cause of death, he or she will report the death to the coroner. The coroner may then arrange for a **post mortem** examination. This usually happens when the person has died from an unknown cause, from an accident or injury, or from an industrial disease. The coroner may also order a post mortem if the person died during an operation, or under anaesthetic. The consent of relatives to a post mortem is not needed, but they are entitled to be represented by a doctor at the examination. The coroner has an obligation to clearly establish the cause of death if at all possible, and in some circumstances this may be a process which will help set your mind at rest about your relative's death. Sometimes the post mortem may cause a slight delay in the funeral arrangements.

There are no coroners in Scotland and these functions are carried out by a public official called the Procurator Fiscal.

3 If your relative wanted to be an organ donor

If your relative discussed organ donation with you or carried an organ donor card, contact the nearest hospital as soon as you can, so that the organs can be removed quickly or tell the attending doctor. If they die in a hospital or hospice, tell the doctor or ward sister, who can help to make the necessary arrangements. People with certain medical conditions, such as cancer, are not able to donate their organs. Your GP or the hospital staff can discuss this with you.

4 Contact a funeral director

As soon as you have the medical certificate from the doctor, you can go ahead and contact a funeral director. The funeral director will help you decide about the practical arrangements for the funeral, such as:

■ Will your relative's body be buried or cremated? Your relative may have expressed a wish about this, possibly in their Will. (There are some extra forms to be filled in if a person is to be cremated. The funeral director will give you these.)

■ Would you like the body to be kept at home or in a chapel of rest until the funeral?

■ Will there be a funeral service or other non-religious ceremony? (If so, you need to contact the people involved – see point 6.)

■ Would you prefer people to send flowers or make donations to a charity?

It is important to choose a funeral director you feel comfortable with. You can get names of local funeral directors from *Yellow Pages*, or you can ask friends and neighbours whom they would recommend. Funerals can be very expensive, so don't be afraid to ask for two or three written quotations before you decide, and make sure you are clear what is included and what is extra. The difference between quotations could well be considerable. Choose a funeral director who is a member of the British Institute of Funeral Directors or the National Association of Funeral Directors (addresses on page 106 and 111).

People who are on a low income may be able to get help with the cost of a funeral from the Social Fund, as explained on page 91. Social Fund payments for funeral expenses do not have to be repaid by surviving relatives but may be recovered from any money in your relative's estate.

You should also check among your relative's documents to see whether they have paid for their funeral in advance.

5 Contact close relatives and friends

It is a good idea to contact relatives and friends as soon as possible. They will want to give you comfort and support, and they may be able to help you with some of the arrangements.

6 Contact the minister of religion or non-religious organisation

If your relative belonged to a religion, you may wish to contact the minister if you have not already done so. Even if they did not attend a place of worship, they may have wanted a religious funeral. If you don't know an appropriate minister, the funeral director or hospital or hospice chaplain may be able to help.

If you want a non-religious ceremony, a society such as the British Humanist Association or the National Secular Society (addresses on page 106 and 112) may be able to arrange for someone to conduct one, or they can send a form of words that could be used.

Things to do over the next few days

7 Register the death

When someone dies, their death must be registered with the Registrar of Births, Deaths and Marriages for your area within five days. You will find the address in the local telephone directory under 'Registration of births, deaths and marriages'.

You should show the registrar:

- the medical certificate given you by the GP;
- the pink form (Form 100) given you by the coroner (if the death was reported to the coroner, although the coroner often sends it direct to the registrar); and
- your relative's medical card and birth and marriage certificates, if available, and war pension order book, if they had one.

The registrar will also want to know:

- your relative's full name, and their maiden name if it was different;
- the date and place of death;
- their last permanent address;
- where and when they were born;
- what their occupation was and the name and occupation of their spouse;
- whether they were receiving a State Pension or other benefits; and
- if they were married, the date of birth of the surviving spouse.

The registrar should give you:

- a **certificate for burial or cremation** (known as the **green form**) unless the coroner has given you an order for burial (form 101) or a certificate for cremation (form E). You should give this to the funeral director: burial or cremation cannot take place without it;
- a **certificate of registration of death** (form BD8), used for claiming social security benefits; and
- leaflets about widows'/widowers' benefits, if appropriate.

If you go to a register office other than the one for the area where the death took place, these certificates will be sent to you.

The registrar will give you a death certificate only if you ask for one. There is a small charge for each copy. You may need a death certificate for sorting out the Will, or to claim pension and insurance rights. You may wish to ask for several copies as the price increases if you need one later on.

Registering the death in Scotland

In Scotland, a death must be registered within eight days, and it may be registered in the registration office for the district in which the death occurred or in the office for the district where the deceased normally lived (as long as this was in Scotland). The information required by a registrar in Scotland is much the same as in England and Wales with some additional questions about the time of death and other family members including previous spouses. After registration the registrar issues a **certificate of**

registration of death (form 14) which should be given to the funeral director to give to the keeper of the burial ground or to the crematorium. You will also be given a form 334/SI **Registration or notification of death**, for use in claiming social security benefits or for National Insurance purposes. These are both free.

8 Sort out the Will

The person named in the Will as the **executor** is the person responsible for dealing with the money and possessions of the person who has died and distributing them in accordance with the Will. If you are the executor and you feel unable to handle this on your own, you may find it helpful to go to a solicitor (whose fees can be paid out of the estate) or a Citizens Advice Bureau.

Unless the estate is very small, the executor must obtain a **grant of probate** from the probate registry office in order to carry out the instructions in the Will. Probate registries are listed under 'probate' in the business section of the phone book. If there is no probate registry in your phone book, ask the Citizens Advice Bureau or another advice centre. For general enquiries you can phone 0870 241 0109 or look at the Court Service website at www.courtservice.gov.uk

People often pay a solicitor to obtain a grant of probate on their behalf, but if the dead person's affairs are not complicated, it is possible to obtain probate without a solicitor's help. In Scotland, this process is called **confirmation** and the executor should apply to the sheriff court.

If there is no Will, someone (usually the nearest relative) must act as the **personal representative** of the person who has died and obtain **letters of administration** from the probate registry office instead. In Scotland, if there is no Will, the next of kin may have to apply to the local sheriff court to be appointed as **executor dative**.

9 Return personal documents and NHS equipment

Personal documents such as pension book, passport, driving licence, cheque book and credit cards should be returned to the offices which issued them, with a note of explanation and the date of death.

Don't forget to return any NHS equipment on loan to your relative, such as a wheelchair, commode or hearing aid.

10 Dispose of personal belongings

Some people find it very distressing to sort through and dispose of the belongings of someone who has died. If possible, do this with other family members or close friends. You will be able to share your memories of your relative, and you are less likely to throw away a memento which someone else would have treasured.

Many charities are pleased to accept the personal belongings of someone who has died, or you may like to give them away to family and friends. Some firms specialise in cleaning out the homes of people who have died. They usually advertise in the local newspapers in the 'Wanted' section. If your relative has any items that are valuable, you may want to keep these and sell them separately.

For more *i*nformation

i Age Concern Factsheets (see page 120 for details of how to obtain factsheets):

   27 *Planning for a Funeral*

   14 *Dealing With Someone's Estate.*

i Department for Work and Pensions booklet D 49 *What to Do After a Death in England and Wales: A Guide to What You Must Do and the help You Can Get,* available free from social security offices and on the Internet at www.dwp.gov.uk

i Leaflet D49S *What to Do After a Death in Scotland: Practical Advice for Times of Bereavement,* available free from a registration, Citizens Advice Bureau or social security office, or from the Scottish Executive Justice Department, Civil Law Division, Room 2W(R), St Andrews House, Regent Road, Edinburgh EH1 3DG. Tel: 0131 244 3581.

i Contact the **Inland Revenue's Probate and Inheritance Tax Helpline** on 0845 302 0900 (9am–5pm, Monday to Friday; calls charged at local rate).

i *How to Obtain Probate* (PA2), a leaflet with accompanying forms which is available from the local probate registry.

ℹ Inland Revenue leaflet IR45 *What To Do About Tax When Someone Dies.*

ℹ Social security leaflet NP45 *A Guide to Bereavement Benefits.*

Your feelings when someone close to you dies

Everyone has their own way of saying goodbye to someone they were close to. It is usually better to let yourself feel all the painful emotions that come to the surface at this time, rather than thinking you have to show control. Most people feel grief and a sense of loss; but it is not unusual to feel guilt, anger, bitterness, resentment and other negative feelings as well. Sometimes these difficult and contradictory emotions take us by surprise, and they can make us think there is something 'wrong' with our feelings for the person who has died. In fact, grieving is a very personal process, and the feelings we go through, although they may follow a similar pattern, will be different for everybody. There is no 'right' or 'wrong' way of mourning – there is just a way which works for you, and helps you come to terms with your loss.

If you are feeling so unhappy that you just cannot cope, you should be able to get professional help. Your GP is the first person to go to. You may be able to get in touch with a bereavement counsellor through your GP or through a hospice or hospital.

If you are feeling seriously depressed, your GP may refer you to the community mental health nurse or put you in touch with a psychotherapist or psychiatrist. MIND (national address on page 111) also offers and advises about counselling and psychotherapy.

For more *i*nformation

ℹ **CRUSE Bereavement Care** (address on page 108) is an organisation which helps bereaved people. It has local branches in some areas. Phone the national office or look in your local telephone directory.

ℹ **The Lesbian and Gay Bereavement Project** (address on page 110) offers support if you have lost a partner or friend or relative.

Useful addresses

Abbeyfield Society
*Housing association specialising
in bedsitters/flats for older people
in shared houses, with warden and
housekeeper available.*

53 Victoria Street
St Albans
Herts AL1 3UW
Tel: 01727 857536
Website: www.abbeyfield.org.uk

AIDS helplines
Freephone:
0800 567 123 (English – 24 hours)
0800 282 446 (Cantonese –Wednesday 6pm–10pm)
0800 282 445 (Asian – Wednesday 6pm–10pm)
0800 282 447 (Arabic – Wednesday 6pm–10pm)
0800 521 361 (Textphone service for deaf people – daily 10am–10pm)

**Alzheimer Scotland –
Action on Dementia**
*For people caring for someone
with dementia who live in Scotland.*

22 Drumsheugh Gardens
Edinburgh EH3 7RN
Tel: 0131 243 1453
Helpline: 0808 808 3000 (24-hr)
Website: www.alzscot.org.uk

Alzheimer's Society
*Information, support and advice
about caring for someone with
Alzheimer's disease.*

Gordon House
10 Greencoat Place
London SW1P 1PH
Tel: 020 7306 0606
Helpline: 0845 300 336
(8.30am–6.30pm, weekdays)
Website: www.alzheimers.org.uk

Arthritis Care
*Provides information, support,
training, fun and social
contact.*

18 Stephenson Way
London NW1 2HD
Tel: 020 7380 6500 (switchboard)
Freephone Helpline: 0808 800
4050 (12pm–4pm, weekdays)
Website: www.arthritiscare.org.uk

Breast Cancer Care
*Breast cancer information
and support, advice
and counselling.*

Kiln House
210 New Kings Road
London SW6 4NZ
Helpline: 0808 800 6000
(10am–5pm, weekdays &
10am–2pm, Saturdays)
Website:
www.breastcancercare.org.uk

**British Association for Counselling
and Psychotherapy**
*For a list of counselling
services in your area.*

1 Regent Place
Rugby
Warwickshire CV21 2PJ
Tel: 0870 443 5252
Website: www.bacp.co.uk

British Colostomy Association
*Provides advice and support
to patients and relatives.*

15 Station Road
Reading
Berkshire RG1 1LG
Tel: 0118 939 1537
Helpline: 0800 328 4257
Website: www.bcass.org.uk

British Heart Foundation
*Information about all
aspects of heart disease.*

14 Fitzhardinge Street
London W1H 6DH
Tel: 020 7935 0185
Website: www.bhf.org.uk

British Humanist Association
*For someone to conduct a non-
religious funeral ceremony or
a form of words you can use.*

1 Gower Street
London WC1E 6HD
Tel: 020 7079 3580
Website:
www.humanism.org.uk

**British Institute of Funeral
Directors**
*Information about arranging a
funeral and about funeral
directors in your area.*

140 Leamington Road
Coventry CV3 6JY
Tel: 024 7669 7160
Website: www.bifd.org.uk

British Lung Foundation
Information about all
aspects of lung disease.

78 Hatton Garden
London EC1N 8LD
Tel: 020 7831 5831
Website:
www.britishlungfoundation.com

British Red Cross
For advice about arranging
equipment on loan. Local
branches in many areas.

9 Grosvenor Crescent
London SW1X 7EJ
Tel: 020 7235 5454
Website: www.redcross.org.uk

CancerBACUP
Support and information for
people with cancer and
their families.

3 Bath Place
Rivington Street
London EC2A 3JR
Helpline: 0808 800 1234
Website: www.cancerbacup.org.uk

Carers UK
Information and advice if you
are caring for someone. Can put
you in touch with other carers
and carers' groups in
your area.

20–25 Glasshouse Yard
London EC1A 4JT
Tel: 020 7490 8818 (admin)
CarersLine: 0808 808 7777
(10am–12pm & 2pm–4pm,
weekdays)
Website: www.carersonline.org.uk

Citizens Advice
For advice on legal, financial and
consumer matters. A good place to
turn to if you don't know where to
go for help or advice on any subject.

Listed in local telephone directo-
ries, or in the *Yellow Pages*
under 'Counselling and advice'.
Other local advice centres may
also be listed.

Continence Foundation
Advice and information
about who to contact
with continence problems.

307 Hatton Square
16 Baldwin Gardens
London EC1N 7RJ
Tel: 020 7404 6875
Helpline: 0845 345 0165 (nurse
available 9.30am–12.30pm,
weekdays)
Website:
www.continence-foundation.org.uk

Counsel and Care
Advice about remaining at home or about care homes.

Lower Ground Floor
Twyman House
16 Bonny Street
London NW1 9PG
Advice Line: 0845 300 7585
(10am–12.30pm & 2pm–4pm, weekdays)
Website:
www.counselandcare.org.uk

Crossroads – Caring for Carers
Has nearly 200 schemes across England and Wales providing practical support to carers in the home.

10 Regent Place
Rugby
Warwickshire CV21 2PN
Tel: 01788 573653
Website: www.crossroads.org.uk

CRUSE – Bereavement Care
For all types of bereavement counselling and a wide range of publications.

Cruse House
126 Sheen Road
Richmond
Surrey TW9 1UR
Helpline: 0870 167 1677
Website:
www.
crusebereavementcare.org.uk

Diabetes UK
Provides help and support to people diagnosed with diabetes, their families and those who care for them.

10 Parkway
London NW1 7AA
Tel: 020 7424 1000
Careline: 0845 120 2960
Website: www.diabetes.org.uk

Disability Wales
National association of disability groups working to promote the rights, recognition and support of all disabled people in Wales.

Wernddu Court
Caerphilly Business Park
Van Road
Caerphilly CF83 3ED
Tel: 029 2088 7325
Website: www.dwac.demon.co.uk

Disablement Information and Advice Lines (DIAL UK)
For your nearest local group, giving information and advice about disability.

St Catherine's Hospital
Tickhill Road
Doncaster
South Yorkshire DN4 8QN
Tel: 01302 310123
Website: www.dialuk.org.uk

Disabled Living Centres Council
Can tell you where your nearest Disabled Living Centre is – where you can get free information and advice about disability aids and equipment.

Redbank House
4 St Chad's Street
Manchester M8 8QA
Tel: 0161 834 1044
Website: www.dlcc.org.uk

Disabled Living Foundation
Information about aids to help cope with a disability.

380–384 Harrow Road
London W9 2HU
Helpline: 0845 130 9177
(10am–4pm, weekdays)
Website: www.dlf.org.uk

Elderly Accommodation Counsel
National charity offering computerised information about all forms of accommodation for older people, including care homes and hospices, and advice on top-up funding.

3rd Floor
89 Albert Embankment
London SE1 7TP
Helpline: 020 7820 1343
Website: www.housingcare.org

foundations
The national coordinating body for home improvement agencies.

Bleaklow House
Howard Town Mill
Glossop SK13 8HT
Tel: 01457 891909
Website: www.foundations.uk.com

Headway (the Brain Injury Association)
For people who are disabled physically or mentally as a result of a head injury, and their carers.

4 King Edward Court
King Edward Street
Nottingham NG1 1EW
Tel: 0115 924 0800
Website: www.headway.org.uk

Holiday Care Service
For specialist information on
holidays for older or disabled
people and their carers. Has a
database of respite care facilities
in the UK.

7th Floor
Sunley House
4 Bedford Park
Croydon CR0 2AP
Tel: 0845 124 9971
Website: www.holidaycare.org.uk

Hospice Information Service
Information about local
hospices.

St Christopher's Hospice
51–59 Lawrie Park Road
London SE26 6DZ
Tel: 0870 903 3903 (9am–5pm,
weekdays)
Website:
www.hospiceinformation.info

Jewish Care
Social care, personal support
and care homes for
Jewish people.

Stuart Young House
221 Golders Green Road
London NW11 9DQ
Tel: 020 8922 2000
Website: www.jewishcare.org

**Lesbian and Gay Bereavement
Project**
A Will pack is available on
receipt of a large sae.

c/o Healthy Gay Living Centre
40 Borough High Street
London SE1
Tel: 020 7407 3550
Helpline: 020 7403 5969
(7pm–10.30pm)

Macmillan Cancer Relief
Funds Macmillan nurses and
works to improve the quality of life
for cancer patients and their
families through information,
support and grant aid.

89 Albert Embankment
London SE1 7UQ
Tel: 020 7840 7840
Macmillan Cancerline:
0808 808 2020 (9am–6pm,
weekdays)
Website: www.macmillan.org.uk

Marie Curie Cancer Care
Provides inpatient centres and
runs home nursing service for
day and night care.

89 Albert Embankment
London SE1 7TP
Tel: 020 7599 7777
Website: www.mariecurie.org.uk

MIND (National Association for Mental Health)
Information, support and publications about all aspects of mental illness, depression, etc.

15–19 The Broadway
London E15 4BQ
Tel: 020 8519 2122
Infoline: 08457 660 163
(9.15am–5.15pm, weekdays)
Publications: 020 8221 9666
Website: www.mind.org.uk

Motability
Cars and wheelchairs for disabled people.

Goodman House
Station Approach
Harlow
Essex CM20 2ET
Tel: 01279 635666

Multiple Sclerosis Society
Provides a welfare support service for the families of people with multiple sclerosis.

MS National Centre
372 Edgware Road
Staples Corner
London NW2 6ND
Tel: 020 8438 0700
Helpline: 0808 800 8000
Website: www.mssociety.org.uk

National Association of Councils for Voluntary Service (NACVS)
Promotes and supports the work of councils for voluntary service. Or look in your telephone directory to see if there is a local CVS.

Arundel Court
177 Arundel Street
Sheffield S1 2NU
Tel: 0114 278 6636
Website: www.nacvs.org.uk

National Association of Funeral Directors
Offers a code of conduct and a simple service for a basic funeral.

618 Warwick Road
Solihull B91 1AA
Tel: 0121 711 1343
Website: www.nafd.org.uk

National Care Standards Commission (NCSC)
Responsible for inspecting and registering care homes. Contact the head office for details of your local office.

St Nicholas Buildings
St Nicholas Street
Newcastle upon Tyne NE1 1NB
Helpline: 0191 233 3556
(8am–6pm, weekdays)
Website:
www.carestandards.org.uk

111

NHS Direct
First point of contact to find out about NHS services.

Tel: 0845 46 47
Website: www.nhsdirect.nhs.uk

National Secular Society
For assistance with a non-religious ceremony or for someone to conduct one.

25 Red Lion Square
London WC1R 4RL
Tel: 020 7404 3126
Website: www.secularism.org.uk

Office of Care and Protection (Northern Ireland)
If you need to take over the affairs of someone who is mentally incapable in Northern Ireland.

Royal Courts of Justice
PO Box 410
Chichester Street
Belfast BT1 3JF
Tel: 028 9023 5111

Office of the Public Guardian in Scotland (OPG)
Information on Continuing Power of Attorney in Scotland.

Hadrian House
Callendar Road
Falkirk FK1 1XR
Tel: 01324 678300

Parkinson's Disease Society
Support and information for relatives and carers of someone with Parkinson's disease.

215 Vauxhall Bridge Road
London SW1V 1EJ
Tel: 020 7931 8080
Helpline: 0808 800 0303
(9.30am–5.30pm, weekdays)
Website: www.parkinsons.org.uk

Pensions Advisory Service (OPAS)
A voluntary organisation which gives advice and information about occupational and personal pensions and helps sort out problems.

11 Belgrave Road
London SW1V 1RB
Tel: 08456 012 923
Website: www.opas.org.uk

Pension Schemes Registry
Information service for tracing pensions.

PO Box 1NN
Newcastle upon Tyne NE99 1NN
Tel: 0191 225 6316
Website: www.opra.gov.uk/
registry/regmenu.shtml

Public Guardianship Office (PGO)
If you need to take over the
affairs of someone who is
mentally incapable in
England or Wales.

Archway Tower
2 Junction Road
London N19 5SZ
Tel: 020 7664 7300/7000
Enquiry Line: 0845 330 2900
Website: www.guardianship.gov.uk

RADAR (Royal Association for
Disability and Rehabilitation)
Information about aids and
mobility, holidays, sport and
leisure for disabled people.

12 City Forum
250 City Road
London EC1V 8AF
Tel: 020 7250 3222
Website: www.radar.org.uk

Registered Nursing Home
Association
Can give you information about
registered nursing homes in
your area which meet the
standards set by the Association.

15 Highfield Road
Edgbaston
Birmingham B15 3DU
Tel: 0121 454 2511
Freephone: 0800 0740 194
Website: www.rnha.co.uk

Relatives and Residents
Association
Support and advice for the
relatives of people in a care home
or in hospital long-term.

24 The Ivories
6–18 Northampton Street
Islington
London N1 2HY
Helpline: 020 7359 8136

RNIB (Royal National Institute
of the Blind)
Advice and support for people
with sight difficulties.

105 Judd Street
London WC1H 9NE
Tel: 020 7388 1266
Helpline: 0845 766 9999
(9am–5pm, weekdays)
Website: www.rnib.org.uk

RNID (Royal National Institute
for Deaf People)
Advice and support for people
with hearing difficulties.

19–23 Featherstone Street
London EC1Y 8SL
Tel: 020 7296 8000
Helpline: 0808 808 0123
(9am–5pm, weekdays)
Textphone: 0808 808 9000
Website: www.rnid.org.uk

RoSPA (Royal Society for the Prevention of Accidents)
Advice and publications on preventing accidents.

Edgbaston Park
353 Bristol Road
Edgbaston
Birmingham B5 7ST
Tel: 0121 248 2000
Website: www.rospa.com

Samaritans
Someone to talk to if you are in despair.

Tel: 08457 90 90 90 or see your local telephone directory
Website: www.samaritans.org.uk

The Stroke Association
Information if you are caring for someone who has had a stroke.

Stroke House
240 City Road
London EC1V 2PR
Tel: 020 7566 0300
Helpline: 0845 30 33 100
Website: www.stroke.org.uk

Tripscope
A travel information service for older and disabled people.

The Vassall Centre
Gill Avenue
Bristol BS16 2QQ
Helpline: 08457 585641
Website: www.tripscope.org.uk

United Kingdom Home Care Association (UKHCA)
For information about organisations providing home care in your area.

42B Banstead Road
Carshalton
Surrey SM5 3NW
Tel: 020 8288 1551
Website: www.ukhca.co.uk

Women's Royal Voluntary Service (WRVS)
Seeks to help people maintain independence in their own homes and communities, particularly in later life.

Milton Hill House
Milton Hill
Steventon
Abingdon
Oxfordshire OX13 6AD
Tel: 01235 442900
Website: www.wrvs.org.uk

About Age Concern

This book is one of a wide range of publications produced by Age Concern England, the National Council on Ageing. Age Concern works on behalf of all older people and believes later life should be fulfilling and enjoyable. For too many this is impossible. As the leading charitable movement in the UK concerned with ageing and older people, Age Concern finds effective ways to change that situation.

Where possible, we enable older people to solve problems themselves, providing as much or as little support as they need. A network of local Age Concerns, supported by many thousands of volunteers, provides community-based services such as lunch clubs, day centres and home visiting.

Nationally, we take a lead role in campaigning, parliamentary work, policy analysis, research, specialist information and advice provision, and publishing. Innovative programmes promote healthier lifestyles and provide older people with opportunities to give the experience of a lifetime back to their communities.

Age Concern is dependent on donations, covenants and legacies.

Age Concern England
1268 London Road
London SW16 4ER
Tel: 020 8765 7200
Fax: 020 8765 7211
Website:
www.ageconcern.org.uk

Age Concern Scotland
113 Rose Street
Edinburgh EH2 3DT
Tel: 0131 220 3345
Fax: 0131 220 2779
Website:
www.ageconcernscotland.org.uk

Age Concern Cymru
4th Floor
1 Cathedral Road
Cardiff CF11 9SD
Tel: 029 2037 1566
Fax: 029 2039 9562
Website:
www.accymru.org.uk

Age Concern Northern Ireland
3 Lower Crescent
Belfast BT7 1NR
Tel: 028 9024 5729
Fax: 028 9023 5497
Website:
www.ageconcernni.org

Other books in this series

The Carers Handbook series has been written for the families and friends of older people. It guides readers through key care situations and aims to help readers make informed, practical decisions. All the books in the series:

- are packed full of detailed advice and information;
- offer step-by-step guidance on the decisions which need to be taken;
- examine all the options available;
- are full of practical checklists and case studies;
- point you towards specialist help;
- are fully up to date with recent guidelines and issues; and
- draw on Age Concern's wealth of experience.

Choices for the carer of an elderly relative
Marina Lewycka
£6.99 0-86242-375-9

Caring for someone at a distance
Julie Spencer-Cingöz
£6.99 0-86242-367-8

Caring for someone with dementia
Jane Brotchie
£6.99 0-86242-368-6

Caring for someone with depression
Toni Battison
£6.99 0-86242-389-9

Caring for someone with cancer
Toni Battison
£6.99 0-86242-382-1

Caring for someone with a sight problem
Marina Lewycka
£6.99 0-86242-381-3

Caring for someone with a hearing loss
Marina Lewycka
£6.99 0-86242-380-5

Caring for someone with arthritis
Jim Pollard
£6.99 0-86242-373-2

Caring for someone with a heart problem
Toni Battison
£6.99 0-86242-371-6

Caring for someone with diabetes
Marina Lewycka
£6.99 0-86242-374-0

Caring for someone who has had a stroke
Philip Coyne with Penny Mares
£6.99 0-86242-369-4

Caring for someone with an alcohol problem
Mike Ward
£6.99 0-86242-372-4

Caring for someone who is dying
Penny Mares
£6.99 0-86242-370-8

Caring for someone with memory loss
Toni Battison
£6.99 0-86242-358-9

Publications from Age Concern Books

Staying Sane: Managing the Stress of Caring
Tanya Arroba and Lesley Bell
The aim of this book is to increase the positive rewards associated with caring and demystify the topic of stress. Complete with case studies and checklists, the book helps carers to develop a clear strategy towards dealing positively with stress.
£14.99 0-86242-267-1

Your Rights: A Guide to Money Benefits for Older People
Sally West
A highly acclaimed annual guide to the State benefits available to older people. Contains current information on State Pensions, means-tested benefits and disability benefits, among other matters, and provides advice on how to claim.
For further information please telephone 0870 44 22 120.

Your Taxes and Savings: A Guide for Older People
Paul Lewis
Explains how the tax system affects older people over retirement age, including how to avoid paying more than necessary. The information about savings and investments covers the wide range of opportunities now available and is updated annually.
For further information please telephone 0870 44 22 120.

Using Your Home as Capital
Cecil Hinton and David McGrath
This best-selling book for homeowners, updated annually, gives a detailed explanation of how to capitalise on the value of your home and obtain a regular additional income.
For further information please telephone 0870 44 22 120.

If you would like to order any of these titles, please write to the address below, enclosing a cheque or money order for the appropriate amount (plus £1.99 p&p for one book; for additional books please add 75p per book up to a maximum of £7.50) made payable to Age Concern England. Credit card orders may be made on 0870 44 22 120. Books can also be ordered online at www.ageconcern.org.uk/shop

Age Concern Books
Units 5 and 6
Industrial Estate
Brecon
Powys LD3 8LA

Bulk order discounts

Age Concern Books is pleased to offer a discount on orders totalling 50 or more copies of the same title. For details, please contact Age Concern Books on Tel: 0870 44 22 120.

Customised editions

Age Concern Books is pleased to offer a free 'customisation' service for anyone wishing to purchase 500 or more copies of the title. This gives you the option to have a unique front cover design featuring your organisation's logo and corporate colours, or adding your logo to the current cover design. You can also insert an additional four pages of text for a small additional fee. Existing clients include many of the biggest names in British industry, retailing and finance, the trades unions, educational establishments, the statutory and voluntary sectors, and welfare associations. For full details, please contact Sue Henning, Age Concern Books, Astral House, 1268 London Road, London SW16 4ER. Fax: 020 8765 7211. Email: hennings@ace.org.uk

Visit our website at www.ageconcern.org.uk/shop

Age Concern Information Line/ Factsheets subscription

Age Concern produces more than 45 comprehensive factsheets designed to answer many of the questions older people (or those advising them) may have. These include money and benefits, health, community care, leisure and education, and housing. For up to five free factsheets, telephone: 0800 00 99 66 (7am–7pm, seven days a week, every day of the year). Alternatively you may prefer to write to Age Concern, FREEPOST (SWB 30375), ASHBURTON, Devon TQ13 7ZZ.

For professionals working with older people, the factsheets are available on an annual subscription service, which includes updates throughout the year. For further details and costs of the subscription, please contact Age Concern at the above address.

Index

We hope that this publication has been useful to you. If so, we would very much like to hear from you. Alternatively, if you feel that we could add or change anything, then please write and tell us, using the following Freepost address: Age Concern, FREEPOST CN1794, London SW16 4BR.

Personal directory

Fill in the phone numbers for your relative as soon as you can –
provided that your relative is happy that you should have them –
and keep in a safe place. It is unlikely that all these numbers will
be relevant to your relative.

	Name/contact	*Telephone number*
Next-door neighbours		
Friends and relatives who live nearby		
GP		
Community nurse		
Community mental health nurse		
Ambulance service		
Hospital (main switchboard)		
Hospital social worker		
Hospital occupational therapist		
Social services department (main switchboard)		
Social services area team		

	Name/contact	*Telephone number*

Social worker

Key worker

Social services occupational therapist

Home care assistant (home help)

Personal care assistant

Age Concern (local group)

Voluntary care organisation

Community transport

Church minister

Private care agency

Private nursing agency

Council housing department (main switchboard)

Local housing management office (for council tenants)

Home improvement agency

Care home

Other useful numbers